EXTENDING THE PLAY
*Business Sustainability for a Next
Generation Economy*

TERRY SHIRING, MBA

DEDICATION

This book is dedicated to God my heavenly Father and to my talented wife
Theresa who is my angel on earth.

CONTENTS

INTRODUCTION

Performance is not a concept, it should be in the DNA of every corporation or start-up business that strives to succeed. At times, performance gets lost in the fog of the day-to-day business wars. The competitive spirit to establish the high water mark against the competition diminishes and is replaced by consistent mediocrity. The desire to be the best, tires under the strain of consistent pressure to benchmark your business as the model of excellence. Unintentional as it may be, your strategy and objectives may not be in alignment with the human capital needed to achieve these goals. Conversely, the human capital that you have retained at your company may be exceptional performers; however, your strategies, goals, and objectives are not being communicated properly in order to fully utilize this tremendous asset.

If you do not know where you are going any road can take you there; however, in the business world it takes great leadership and performance from the C-Suite down to navigate the path to brand your business model as the best in the global arena. In order to accomplish this you will need an excellent team of performers and leaders that will prolong the lifecycle of your corporation. This does not take a rocket scientist to understand or accomplish; however, at times this concept runs interference with the forward thinking processes to effectively lead a business. Entrepreneurially speaking, new start up businesses may not have the budget or experience levels to employ topnotch talent, or hire consultants to conduct training programs that will empower your business to reach those high water marks. Consistent examination of your bottom line and return on investment is generally centered on financial return and capital equipment investment; however, at times budgets are trimmed in the area of human capital investment that should be considered your most important acquisition. Incorporating training and organizational effectiveness processes will enhance the quality of your organizational culture with thought leadership processes, and continuous quality improvement strategies that will brand and develop your business model. The dynamics and processes of this book are evolutionary in their style and delivery as your business model continues to change through turbulent economic times. If the lifecycle of your business is essential, you will need the performance and development of your Human Capital to extend the play.

This book will be an excellent tool for all corporate and human resources executives as well as required reading for a university business curriculum.

TERRANCE SHIRING

1 GPS FOR YOUR SUCCESS
THE MISSION STATEMENT

There it hangs, neatly shined, properly matted, and placed in the most ornate framing suitable for a Vatican art collection. The corporate Mission Statement, the prodigy of executive think tanks, woven with the majesty of the best word artisans in the business. This statement clearly portrayed at the corporate entrance, empowers all who enter with the message of customer excellence, the promise of strategic vision, and social consciousness. Unknown to most executives who steer the helm of corporate global prominence is that this mission statement should be the pro-active genesis of their competitive advantage. Most corporate mission statements are pieced together as a public relations approach strategy, a commercial if you will, to set the profitable pathway in their business arena. The importance, significance, and crafting of this mission statement should only be conceived and crafted by the collective minds of the CEO and President of the company after the objective and strategic goals of the company have been established, and everyone within the organization has been informed of the strategic goals and initiatives of the corporation. The ability to effectively communicate the 'vision' is what sets leaders apart from mere managers. Generally, the mission statement is crafted in reaction to market trends or changing cultural philosophies with very little input from executive management into the implementation of the strategies that will get the results and promises made to the target markets.

I have considered the importance of strategic planning, prior to conceptualizing and constructing the mission statement from my business ventures and observations of corporations at work. From front line receptionists to managerial staffing, it appears that in most cases the message on the mission statement was not conveyed to all hands on deck. I have seen multi-million dollar customers greeted without a smile from the front desk receptionist, executive phone calls going to the proverbial voicemail due to a lethargic executive administrator, and even important client meetings delayed well beyond the scheduled appointment time.

My vision of a problem free utopian corporate environment is not the purpose of this book, but it is one of vision alignment and empowerment to all employees to understand and carry out this vision to increase your competitive advantage. In Asian culture, there is a philosophy that one small change can have universal ripples. We are now in a market of global prominence and universality of opportunity. You would never write a forward for a business book without knowing the author or reading the content. This could dramatically tarnish your image in the business arena if the philosophies and content in the book were in contrast or not in alignment with your ideologies. The same principle applies to the mission statement. You cannot construct the mission statement until the vision and strategies have been established by the CEO and communicated to the top line executives throughout the entire organization. This systematic approach not only prevents mixed messaging, but also aligns and establishes a clear and concise business plan that will drive and increase your competitive advantage in the marketplace. Secondly, this vision needs to be shared with all employees in order to set goals and expectations, as well as, establishing a culture of inclusiveness and performance expectations. When there is a shared vision of purpose with all human capital, this is the genesis of a socially engineered culture of teamwork at all levels and not one of a supporting cast with many leading roles.

The mission statement should also promote a philosophy of social consciousness and awareness that transmits a polished image of care and responsiveness to the social and ecological needs of the community and environs in which you operate. When the short and long term strategic goals are established with a vision, direction, and purpose, this will result in crafting a mission statement with more then mere words, but a carefully quilted mosaic comprised of a plan of action that has already provided your organization with a track record of a clear competitive advantage. Your mission statement needs to be your north star, your beacon so to speak. The mission statement is also a tool that can be a challenge to your company or business to live up to the expectations that you set for your business and transparently projected to your customers. When constructing your mission statement focus only on your core competencies and social and customer concerns. Remember, this is not fiction this is your shingle your brand and model that you are selling to your customers. Allow me now to extend to all businesses, companies, and corporations some very viable tips for completing a mission statement. To successfully construct an effective mission statement model, the following steps should be applied:

1. Know your brand, your products and services, and what you want your organization to achieve.
2. Design your blueprint for strategy and goal attainment.
3. Implement a commitment and concern for employees and external customers.
4. Express social and environmental consciousness and commitment to the communities where you conduct your business.
5. Most important say what you mean and above all do what you say. A mission statement is also a statement of ethics and responsibility adopted by corporate governance. Always produce both ends of the equation to obtain the desired results.

The above-mentioned steps will surely provide a mapping of ingredients that will need to be positioned into your mission statement to effectively highlight to your business community not only your products and services, but your commitment to the community. This is a very important ingredient as social consciousness is imperative in the current business environment. The environment in a next generation economy is one of corporate responsibility and commitment to the community development. In business, it is a two way street, similar to that of forestry, when you cut down a tree, plant one as well. Replenishing the community with charitable contributions, environmental services, and resourcefulness in their use of the factors of production makes for good business. Another great idea is to have a genuine concern for the growth and development of the youth in the community with financially assisting programs that will educate and grow great citizens and leaders. Of course, all this needs done according to the size and financial stability of your business, however, there are always opportunities to assist and participate in giving back what the community is providing you. Lastly, MEAN AND DO WHAT YOU SAY in your mission statement since you will surely be called on it from time to time. Backsliders have a very difficult time of looking at themselves in the mirror of the community, and any hope of longevity will surely fade into haze.

2 EXTENDING THE PLAY

Watching a great football game on a Sunday afternoon is a very relaxing habit of mine. My enjoyment comes from the many strategies and plays that I see from both teams as the game proceeds forward. The closer the score of the game, the more you can see the strategic thinking and determination dripping from the faces of the coaches and players on the sidelines. When you hear the cracking of hands as the huddle breaks and the players take the line of scrimmage, my attention is drawn to the quarterback as he surveys the field like a general in combat. After viewing the combat zone, he at times has to call an audible or change the play at the last minute as the opposing teams' defense makes adjustments. Even at times, the best play breaks down after the players running their routes are well covered and the quarterback has to scramble to avoid the sack as he looks for other opportunities to cross the goal line. While watching one particular game, the opposing defense was strategically covering every play, and the quarterback had to scramble out of the pocket to make something happen. Then with fourth quarter heroics, the quarterback scrambled out of the pocket from side to side eluding tacklers at every corner and launched a 50-yard pass down field that went in for a touchdown. The color commentator stated emphatically to his colleague, what a performance by the quarterback, that touchdown would have never happened if he did not have the athletic ability to scramble and extend the play. That statement by the color commentator stayed with me long after the game was over.

As a Human Resources consultant, where analytics and performance metrics are a major part of my business, I began to think about that statement extending the play. Is that not exactly what we look at in the day-to-day modeling of our business as we attempt to benchmark against the competition. Do we not look for ways to extend our play and promote the longevity of our business lifecycle? Doing business in a global marketplace has raised the bar on being competitive at the level required to be successful. Metaphorically speaking, Darwin's theory of survival of the fittest has gone beyond the bounds of the human species surviving in an ever-changing environment. We can now apply that same principle to the ever-changing business arena as well. Many businesses and corporations can vision success and conjure up images of the steps that are necessary to achieve this, however, with fierce competition in the marketplace on a global scale, even their greatest plans are laid to waste when forward thinking performers, and great leadership is not in the mix. This process begins with a transparency of strategy throughout the corporation or business from the C-Suite on down. The left hand needs to know what the right hand is doing especially the Human Resources Department who provides the plasma in the form of human capital to successfully run the business. The C-Suite defines the strategy, establishes a business model, sets the benchmark standards for this work of art to take place, and then disconnects from the Human Resources Department who is the artist of this canvas. Let me explain further to eliminate any misconceptions regarding this theory. I have heard many top-level executives state that they give their Human Resources Department complete autonomy with their hiring decisions and practices. This is fine in and of itself, however, when the strategy needs to meet with sound performers, is your human resources staff equipped with the proper talent and professionals to identify, interview, and hire the right talent? I have witnessed the best-laid strategies and plans go by the wayside because of poor recruiting, interviewing, and selection processes. In the strategic mission of the company, the equation has to encompass straight-line talent in every single department especially in the area of human resources who is responsible for supplying the talent through the pipeline. Each day, senior executives have full schedules and cannot be responsible for every department, however, they need to place responsible leaders in these roles, or the strategy is a plan to fail.

Extending the play, performance, and lifecycle of your company, cannot be sub-planted with consistent mediocrity of poor talent management. Hiring of top-level talent to manage this vital area of human resources will produce positive results that will alleviate negative outcomes for your bottom line. In turn, they will provide your business with talent management solutions on a global level that will raise the bar against your competitive arena. There are many factors in the matrix organization that needs to be taken into consideration when bench marking your business against the competition. Inevitably, we need to start with senior and middle management. The twenty first century business model has become far more complex then the models of the past. Computerized technological software programs that run aggregate production systems with speed and accuracy have replaced specialized mechanistic labor. The catalyst of this environment has been the continuous supply and demand of expectations in the current society, which demands a consistent supply of high quality diverse product streams. To meet this demand, companies have to bring on the talent and leaders who will consistently meet these expectations. This is where the corporate complexities come into play with the ever-changing corporate culture. As I previously stated, the company has evolved from mechanistic standardization in a domestic market to one of sophisticated technological models in a global arena. Managers are now required to lead individuals and teams from diverse countries and cultural backgrounds into being high-level performers and contributors. Management now has additional functional requirements such as forward thinking, thought leadership, culturally sensitive and emotional intelligent leaders. Emotional Intelligence and situational management leadership abilities meeting with a diverse cultural workforce has supplanted the mechanistic autocratic style of management that was the titan of industrial America. Change management within the corporate arena has reached critical mass proportions, as change has been the only constant. Retooling and remodeling of the corporate brand takes place daily as competition becomes fierce and lifecycle preservation takes center stage.

Extending your play in the strategic initiatives battle that is taking place in the global market now requires companies to hire leaders and strategic thinkers who are multi-dimensional in their analytical and forward thinking processes. Managers must also advance integrated team building procedures and promote continuous quality improvement measures to utilize the full potential of their employees, staff and line supervisors. In a diverse global hiring market, the ability to penetrate the barriers of cultural and ethnical communication are essential qualities that must continuously be trained, developed, and updated with your management and employee team to eliminate any performance gaps in the strategy. Failure to achieve this level of talent will certainly mark the demise of your business. This responsibility lies strictly in the hands of your Human Resources Department, and that is why I emphatically state that this area needs highly qualified not quantified employees to provide the human capital to meet your corporate strategy. Diversity adds even more complexity to the issue, as selecting talent from the rich reserves of cultural backgrounds and perspectives requires a wisdom and knowledge that surpasses the standardized hiring practices of the past. Success can be contagious within your business by following and acquiring these principles and making them part of your intra-business model. Reading the great success stories of winning teams in football, basketball, and other sports venues will demonstrate a common thread that runs through the mosaic, and that is having a visionary leader aligned with a great recruiting team. The beauty from this process is that success continues to attract star performers who want to be part of your success, and companies who thrive on this process will continue to generate lifecycle longevity. This process continues to drive itself and reaps a bounty of great returns. The ROI funnel continues to reap great returns as this process continues to feed off its success. This is a very organic process and can run like a well-oiled machine, however, the caveat is that latency will not thrive in a Next Generation economy. Consistent monitoring of the external market and keeping leadership and quality performers in your internal environment is the key driver.

3 PERFORMANCE STRATEGIES FOR YOUR BUSINESS LIFECYCLE

For many businesses, performance is a strategic objective highlighted on a mission statement, with very little procedures put into place to gain that necessary competitive advantage. This type of business attitude is a plan to fail, and one that will quickly diminish the lifecycle of your business. We are now in a very turbulent economy and business market, where businesses are being tossed on the waves of the economic storm and some are taking on water very quickly. It is essential, now more than ever, to develop a performance plan that will model and brand your business to navigate strategically the seas of a global business arena.

Performance is not a set of standardized procedures passed on to every front line manager to adopt and transmit to their subordinates; performance is an attitude and engine that drives success. There is no side stepping true performance measures, and unlike our interstate highways, there is no easy on or off exits. Performance is hard work that must be part of your business or corporate chemistry. Your management and training team cannot soft sell this strategy to your employee base with quick fix anecdotes and subtle nuances. With proper maintenance and consistent monitoring, while keeping your finger on the pulse of your competitive environment, a successful performance approach will drive your business for many years. Performance should be a pro-active culture in your business that will set the pathway to benchmarking your company, not only as the standard for your industry, but as the magnificence of customer satisfaction that sets your competitive advantage at a level superior to the typical business arena.

Executives may ask where does performance begins. Performance begins with the receptionist at your front desk. Wow! this is revolutionary thinking. What does the receptionist have to do with the performance of the company? Answer, everything. The receptionist is the signature of your company, the face of your business, and the welcome mat of your mission statement. If one link is broken on even the strongest chain, there is no outside force that will keep the unity together. There can never be a disconnect between managers, staff, and line management. Every strategic plan and goal of the company must be transmitted to subordinates from the top to entry level. Let me add some logic for thought. A perspective client/customer calls into the receptionist at the front desk to do business with your company possibly a multi-million dollar client/customer. A simple mistake such as a lethargic attitude, lack of attention to detail, or transfer to the wrong department (please do not do this, ouch) will be the catalyst in sending Mr. Million Dollar customer in search of. That is why I insist on the theory that everybody is a star.

Performance needs to be planned, developed, and assessed on an aggregate level inclusive of every department and functional procedure in alignment with the strategic goals and initiatives set forth. We cannot only assess the employees of these departments and functional units, management must be audited as to how they are performing in the process of actualizing and carrying out the strategies and goals as they plan and delegate duties to their subordinates. Performance is a continuous process of thinking, rethinking, inventing, reinventing, thought leadership, and situational management based on the continuous changes that are reflective in the current business environment. Communication, leadership development, and organizational training must be the adhesive tape of your organization that meets the challenges of an ever-changing market in a consumer driven business arena. Performance must also be measured and managed by managers and supervisors that possess a six sense of the business climate, market trends, and the consumer driven needs of a market that continues to have an insatiable appetite for new products and services. Managers must also possess a high degree of emotional intelligence in order to facilitate change and situational business decisions that occur frequently and unexpectedly. There is no blueprint to manage these turn on a dime situations, just the need for good quality managers who have the ability to manage conflict and changes, as well as the ability to acquire proactive and forward thinking processes. Critical thinking and thought leadership abilities are the catalyst that prolongs the lifecycle of your company, and maintains a steady finger on the pulse of the business environment. Performance is not the genesis of this entire process. It is the result of a carefully crafted strategic plan, market analysis, and the thinking outside the box process. This will enable you to present your company with a performance plan, which will brand your business as the leader in your arena as well as combat the fog of business war. With this performance plan there must also be a metrics system put into place that will enable managers to measure the results efficiently to ensure that desired results are meeting the strategic plan. Remember, you cannot manage what you cannot measure. Performance enhancement for your business is a multi-faceted composite of planning and analyzing the internal and external environment of your business arena.

Beginning with the external environment for performance execution, the strategic initiatives and planning must be facilitated on a global think tank basis. Residing primarily in a domestic market for business, growth and development casts a shadow of a small footprint not suitable for the aggressive business arena in the present day culture. When the global planning process begins, the genesis of the planning should be to determine what global markets you are seeking to pursue. A business must consider the internal and external factors of the country they are looking to do business with as part of the performance planning. A carefully designed and structured SWOT analysis must be implemented prior to stepping into the global business arena. This is an important step to take to examine the strengths, weaknesses, threats, and opportunities that your company will engage in to become competitive in the global arena internally and externally. This must be done prior to establishing your strategic objectives and goals. What contingency plans are set in place as your company sets their sights on the global business arena? Many unique situations arise on the global terrain that can disable your business performance. Are you ready to face these challenges? Are you flexible in the business arena to absorb the shock of a worldwide financial collapse, a fiscal cliff, or an overnight change in a foreign government that is no longer favorable to foreign interest? Some key concepts to explore are the taxation laws, are they favorable to your business environment? In obtaining employees to facilitate your overseas operations, will you export domestic employees, or will you put into place an expatriate hiring initiative? How will the cultures cross, taking into consideration customs, practices, and religious beliefs? Government stabilization in foreign markets is a very important consideration that needs to be addressed prior to engaging in business activity. Your business has to define if relationships between the populous and the country you are seeking to do business with are on good terms or if coup attempts are possible that could disrupt your operations and produce drastic negative results. This also ties in very well with the financial considerations that must be explored in doing business on a global level. Countries lacking a stabilized government that are consistently in strife will produce cataclysmic negative effects on the currencies and financial makeup of that market. In addressing the financial considerations of entering global markets, one must be on constant vigilance of currency fluctuations internationally and domestically, as well as, destabilizing economic factors in the global business arena. Will your business have to entertain hedging opportunities to offset currency fluctuations in the market, or will you produce and ship raw materials and finished product to your global site without the concern of currency fluctuations? With those concerns stated, it is clearly visible that there is much more then just training and strategic planning procedures that define your performance initiatives. The competitive nature of the current business is not a very forgiving environment. You either compete or face the Darwin theory of Natural Selection, the survival of the fittest, and in order to address this competitive environment your business must be intellectually, financially, and emotionally fit. You are going to need performance enhancing human capital to get you there. Strategic planning, metrics design, and thought leadership are all the by products of human capital investment. Your hiring processes must not just produce bodies, but creative minds that can also be empowered to produce leaders and responsible employees. Let me emphasize responsible employee selection. At all levels of your organization, your selected employees must be willing to fulfill their particular function as if they were co-owners of the business. They must be positive and responsible employees in order to be productive to your business. On a domestic or global level, your human capital is the catalyst that drives your business. As I stated in a previous chapter, it is the oil that drives the business engine and the defining measure that defines performance. I have discussed many strategies and procedures in order to defy ordinary in performance, and gain that competitive edge, however, what steps are necessary to measure and meet these standards to ensure successful continuous quality improvement? The aggregate strategy of the company must blend into the job descriptions and functions of each position according to the vital standards that need to be achieved. My philosophy is that no position in the company is exempt from performance monitoring and standards met auditing. Always bear in mind that many kingdoms have crumbled due to a tactical error of the gatekeeper. In the current business market, job functions and descriptions need restructuring and revising to meet the demands of the international marketplace. The international market is a huge cloak that covers the entire global surface from capitalist driven economies to emerging markets each with their own culture and political demands. Doing business within these environments is not business as usual, and the proverbial gatekeeper cannot fall asleep at the corporate entrance, nor can status quo or steady the wheel be the call from the watchtower. Talent management can never be compartmentalized in the aggressive business market that we are experiencing today. Talent search is like a college draft day as companies scramble for the brightest and the best to secure and shore up their competitive advantage, and benchmark their corporate image. Strategies are now focusing on a global spectrum, mixing and blending cross-cultural talent into local and global entities to bring those strategies into fruition are becoming more complex. Cruise control works well on a straight highway, however, business is no longer a straight highway, and in the current market there is always going to be twists and turns to navigate. In order to remain competitive, companies need to hire and retain top quality performers by providing continuous training and development programs and performance enhancing procedures for quality checks to remain consistent, timely, and efficient. Once again, this is where many companies put on the cruise control and do not want to invest the time, resources, or the efforts as part of their business model. The functions of each job description must be redefined and restructured to meet the ever-changing demands and intellectual capabilities needed to achieve success in a domestic and international market. Human Resources is the watchtower who needs to keep an eye on the changing marketplace and make adjustments in real time to place the best talent in all positions. Talent management is a very crucial role in the company that requires a very keen set of minds and tremendous analytical abilities in order to provide the company with the human resources necessary to successfully meet and exceed the corporate strategic goals and objectives. In Chapter 8, I will discuss how to successfully develop a metrics auditing and performance review process to ensure quality standards. The business arena speaks quite emphatically that in the competitive marketplace talent management must consist of hiring and retaining human capital that will be forward thinking leaders, which will be the core competency of success in modeling and driving the lifecycle of the business. I could not agree more with this philosophy; however, I would like to inject one caveat into the mix. Hiring forward thinking talent is only one part of the equation, they must also have an understanding of how people think and react from co-workers to external customers on a global level in order to have complete organizational effectiveness. The forward thinking process must not be self-indulgent and strictly for corporate profiteering and return on investment purposes. Only balancing one part of the equation will not promote longevity.

A consistent focus on the changing trends in the thinking processes and needs of the internal and external client base will secure a business model of successful branding and lifecycle advancement. In order to enhance performance and defy the ordinary your corporate philosophy will need to focus on the ever-changing needs of the customers, and the hierarchy needs of your human capital as they progress and develop into leadership roles. In the current business world, there has been much reflection and philosophical studies on Generation Y and Generation X cultural attributes, and how they play into the work lifecycle of human capital and performance planning. The objective and strategic planning sessions in the corporate suites from a hiring and staffing perspective have proceeded to be more of an endearment to cultural fitness at times with less concentration on training and development for performance. The work life balance has certainly evolved over the last decade, and there are certainly issues that need addressed and discussed, however, they cannot spill over to the corporate road map for success. Human Capital development comprises of providing the employee with the adequate tools and training to develop and become a successful employee on the job, not only for returns on the bottom line but to assist the employee to achieve their hierarchy of needs. A business must make this of utmost importance while working these philosophies into their life balance as well. I believe that many businesses have butted heads with the work life balance equation and conservatively planned for life balance while placing minimal forward thinking processes on the performance end of the equation. We know from our math days in basic accounting that you cannot force balance a statement without leaving the error on the sheet or trying to cover for it; the end result is that there is still an error left to reconcile. To sum it up you need to concentrate on keeping the company solvent and growing, while keeping your eye on the life balance needs and performance mentoring of your employees. Like a great artist, this needs to be a well-crafted piece not all one shade. Performance should never reach a stage of critical mass in your business. Aggregate level competition in the global arena is now a very real and serious trend that all businesses need to focus on with continuous quality improvement, performance management, and quality talent acquisition.

4 A REVOLUTIONARY CONCEPT
"Minimum Human Capital → Maximum Results"

To present in historical relations the ultimate importance of acquiring top-level talent for increased performance and competitive advantage, I will borrow some reflections from one of my talks on the leadership qualities of George Washington. The campaign at Valley Forge was a very decisive point of the Revolutionary War. It was a poignant moment of strategic management, empowerment, and resolve. We could say that the Revolutionary War introduced the concepts of working lean. The Continental Army was decimated with disease, poor equipment, low volumes of human capital, and very low morale. Washington was trying to establish a campaign that would band together a group of soldiers that would be able to continue the war. Lack of shelter, scarce provisions, low morale, and diseases ravaging the camp, were just a few hurdles he had to overcome. Most businesses at this point would call it quits, and this is where great leaders and real talent step up to the challenge. That is why I cannot emphasize enough that no expense should be spared when acquiring great talent, and this is what the 'fit' should be.

During these times of great economic uncertainty, complimented with a punctuating reset economy that is disturbing business tranquility on a global level, a certain amount of risk must be challenged to gain a competitive footprint. Your business will need talented managers and employees to get you there. George Washington had to define and refine the purpose and reasoning of the mission statement to his troops. He had to reinvigorate and empower a sick, lean, and decimated force to see through his eyes the vision and purpose of his strategies and purpose of the mission that needed to be completed. At times in the business world, when competition is squeezing you on all sides, and a faltering economy has taken its' toll on your capital liquidity to acquire and maintain the factors of production, you must maintain a very upbeat and optimistic outlook to remain in the arena. Having a myopic vision at this time would be catastrophic. Many companies have a great exit plan, a strategy when failure and despair is casting its shadow. Some companies even have a great plan to fail. What is this you say, a plan to fail? Well, yes! They invest more strategic thinking into what to do if they fail then a strategic plan for success. Generally, this is because running a successful organization requires time, planning, and talent. Some have the great mental energy to succeed, conversely the physical stamina and 12 to 15 hour days wear thin. I will group together the planning and talent requirements to conduct a successful business, since you need to have great talent and leadership to proceed with great planning and strategy. Talent can be costly, so at times the business decides to proceed with the status quo. Now one may say that George Washington did not have great talent with his troops at Valley Forge, in spite of this, he had great leadership skills that produced tremendous results. Great leaders can take minimum talent and produce amazing maximum outcomes. In the present day, global market on-boarding of diverse talent is of the utmost importance, and George Washington understood this quite well at Valley Forge. The British were well-equipped, very regimented, and disciplined fighting force who were accustomed to doing battle in foreign lands. The young Continental Army was not as regimented or equipped to feel confident going into such a massive battle especially against the mighty British forces. The Prussians during the same century period were like the British as well. The discipline and focused attitude that was engrained in their training was the element that consummated their success. The great Baron De Steuben, a Prussian soldier and trainer of the troops at Valley Forge, instilled a tremendous amount of discipline into his art of war training methodology. He clearly understood, like the Prussians that in the fog of war discipline and focus is what's needed. During these tough economic times, many businesses are entering into the fog of the competitive business war. Strong leaders, instilling focus and discipline, as well as the creative spirit to reinvent legacy techniques into new methodologies, products, services, and ideas is what clears the fog and increases competitive advantage. I cringe when I hear businesses advertising for a cattle call of human capital to just show up at a specific location to work on a particular project. The classified ad then goes on to say no experience necessary, no college required. I sure hope that they will have a George Washington leader present who will mold and shape this raw talent into a fine tuned production team or chaos will take over. Unbelievably, this is what happens in many businesses who feel that they can get by on quantifying and not qualifying their human capital. Would this be the 'fit' in your business or any business? With so much talent coming from many great universities and colleges, why on so many occasions are they lost in a resume abyss? There is a simple answer to this equation. The management or leaders of the recruiting department must have the forward thinking, perception, and strategic mentality that was necessary in the mind of George Washington to select and qualify talent that can be fashioned into leaders and strategic partners in the overall corporate plan. This does not require a rocket scientist it just entails a clear and concise redefining of the 'fit' in your organization. George Washington did not have all the modern day resources that we have in the business arena to secure and acquire talent. He did not have the internet, or sophisticated software packages to assist him in testing and training his troops. What he did have was the desire, discipline, and focus to bring out the best of his troops, and to create and train leaders to deliver the strategy that was necessary for competitive advantage and ultimate victory. George Washington could have possibly been the founder of emotional intelligence and situational management without even knowing it. The battle and fog of war is no different then the daily battle that takes place in the competitive field of the business arena. George Washington had to be creative, resourceful, and emotionally resilient in order to make situational management decisions at a moments notice. He had to be the eyes and mind of the enemy in order to execute the X's and O's on the battlefield, and draw up strategies that would give the Continental Army a competitive advantage. On a moments notice his intended strategies had to transition into an emergent strategy. This was not a solo flight, and to finalize the execution of his strategies he needed to shape and mold troops that were at the least a group of novices whose only armor was determination and desire. George Washington had to maximize these attributes to their fullest potential, and convert and transform these qualities into building leaders and managers on the battlefield. Under the most extreme of circumstances under the leadership of George Washington, this group of human capital had to take personal responsibility for their individual roles as well as their comrades, while engaging in one of the fiercest battles on American soil next to the Civil War.

This is why an extremely functional human resources team is a vital component of your corporation. They must select and choose candidates that are emotionally and intellectually sound in judgment as well as one who is willing to be a leader and responsible for their tasks. Regardless of the type of position that you are hiring for, this system must be followed to ensure quality and performance. I would be remiss if I did not mention the fact that when your company or business has made a decision to hire for a particular position, do not make the lethal mistake of foot dragging the process in filling the position. Many talented individuals have been lost to the competition due to lack of decision-making and forward mobility in the hiring process. In the business world, or in personal life, their will always be a Valley Forge to overcome, yet it is the strategies and forward thinking leadership processes that you put into place that will assist your business or private life in dealing with these sudden bumps in the road. It was in this area that George Washington was a true tactical leader. He was quite aware that preparing for war with all the planning involved, still centered on the performance and leadership abilities of his troops (human capital). He was a visionary who was dealing with issues much like businesses in today's economy. Primarily, George Washington had to train and develop a group of diverse cultures and philosophies that were under staffed and under budgeted. As a good leader, he also realized his limitations and had to acquire great European military leaders to assist in disciplining and training his troops. He had to identify the problems at hand, then lead, and guide a multi-cultural staff of employees and professionals to accomplish his objectives. Is this not a reflection on the present business culture that we are coping with today? That is why I insist that your human resources staff needs to be equipped with the adequate talent, training, and budget, in order to recognize and provide the very best in human capital, which will deliver the greatest core competency to your business. Your leaders must also possess the vision to pinpoint the cholesterol in the arteries of your business and replace low performance with a qualified staff of diligent employees. This system of performance measures can be a fluid self-running and viable game plan on an aggregate level that can reap continuous and ongoing rewards.

5 SUCCESSION PLANNING IN A GLOBAL MARKET
Talent Management and Leadership

I can almost hear the strike of a dissonant chord throughout the great harmonic halls of corporate human resources departments that talent management and leadership succession planning requires the proverbial 'fit'. Within the human resources arena, there is a symphony of harmonies, styles, and structures, as well as the required ways of hiring and thinking that may not be the best answer to the process of hiring great talent and leadership succession planning. I have heard through many prescreen interviews and orientations that the company is looking for the right fit to fill this vacancy, to manage this position, to maximize our talent base, and to provide us with the best human capital. Once during a seminar that I delivered, I asked a group of human resources managers and recruiters to explain to me their definition of what the 'fit' is in making a hiring decision a term that is loosely used in the current human resources arena. I was not surprised but amazed at their responses although they kept in harmony with each other. Most responses stated that the 'fit' meant having oneness or fluidity with their corporate culture, and an employee who they thought could jell with the current staff. In no way am I criticizing any human resources professionals, and these answers and responses that I received were all excellent and informative; however, what was missing were responses speaking to intellect, education, a keen sense of business, and leadership capabilities. To maintain a healthy performing corporation and branding your business for successful competitive advantage, your hiring must go well beyond the fit. Many corporate executives believe that physical capital such as equipment, raw materials, and product lines are at the utmost importance, however, without the right human capital to drive and direct the resources the company will not progress.

A very close friend of mine is a classic car enthusiast, and one weekend he invited me to a classic car show. I was extremely impressed at his knowledge as we passed from vehicle to vehicle. In articulate detail, he explained every make and model, down to engine size, capabilities, and faults. Being a novice in auto mechanics, I asked my friend what do you feel sets one car apart from the other? I was quite surprised at his response, the owner. What a compelling and thought provoking response. I was waiting for a carefully crafted and detailed response for each make and model, and I get a briefly worded statement. When I pressed him to explain further he quipped that these cars cannot perform successfully for any length of time without the right owner taking proper care of them to maintain their individual performance levels. This example sums up talent management and performance at the same time. To build a successful and high performing corporation you need to attain and retain talented human capital that will be the high octane of performance. Selecting talent for your organization is definitely a 360-degree process and should never be quantified even for labor-intensive industries. Many industries have a philosophy that the more bodies the better, just so we have enough hands on deck. This concept is a plan to fail regardless of your business line. The genesis of all hiring should begin with the objective and strategic goals that were set forth from the beginning as stated in earlier chapters. The human resource staff needs to communicate these goals in order to ensure that the screening and interviewing processes are in alignment with the corporate philosophies. When you are staffing the administrative, technical, engineering, and labor-intensive positions for your organization, the interviewing processes have to be fine-tuned and structured to secure the correct and most efficient talent needed to gain competitive advantage, and to fulfill the strategic goals of your organization. When the human resources manager schedules a staff meeting to communicate the hiring needs and goals of the organization, this is exactly when the behavioral interviewing processes and job description realignment processes need to be in place. I like to call this process human capital engineering, since the entire process and philosophy of interviewing, and job description alignment is the center of attaining the highest-level of employee performance. Starting with the job description, this needs to be the blueprint for setting the performance expectations for each position in order to achieve the desired results. Careful study and analysis needs to be in place prior to writing the job description as this task is not to be taken lightly. This will be the road map for setting the behavioral interview process in place. Real work life situations as well as situational decision-making should be addressed in the interview. The if-what question and answer session as well as testing the emotional intelligence level of each candidate needs to be structured in a format that will successfully bring to light not only the intelligence level of each candidate, but the situational effectiveness and emotional management aptitude and abilities as well. The interviewer can determine the candidate's talents and emotional intelligence by the candidate's responses to real life work situations, and how they performed and actively addressed each situation. While conducting a successful interview the questions need to read like a Hollywood script, well thought out with a final plot, and all pointed to and aligned with the strategic initiatives and vision of the company. This process will assist in selecting the right candidate the first time avoiding costly turnover, and low employee retention. During this interview process, the expectations of the company and the functional requirements of the position need to be defined and established. Like a great resume, leave no gaps or holes in the interview for the candidate to slip through. Talent management goes far beyond the selection of the right candidate, retaining and building leadership with your human capital as well as packaging compensation plans for competitive advantage needs to have a defined blueprint. Identifying and selecting the right talent for your corporation is a process and not just a systemized outline of steps to utilize when conducting an interview. A candidate must be qualified during the interview by accessing their critical thinking skills and emotional intelligence, and aligning them with the strategic initiatives and goals of the department that they are being considered for. This will help the interviewer establish how each candidate will perform under pressure, or when situations require multi-tasking, and on the spot decision-making. During this part of the interview, do not establish a consistent or established set of questions used from interview to interview. Carefully develop a set of questions prior to the interview that will aid in identifying leadership traits, functional abilities, and the ability to work alone or in teams all for the best interest of the company. Emotional intelligence assessment will assist the interviewer in determining how the candidate will react to working under pressure, the ability to make split second decisions, as well as interacting with other employees and members of management and client groups. The critical thinking assessment is of the utmost importance in determining the cognitive abilities of the candidate to adequately make the correct decision gleaned from assessing and gathering information. This information also assists in determining if the candidate has the ability to properly obtain and identify information collected from the existence of a problem or problem areas that need to be addressed and resolved. Talent management and retention is a very involved process, however, arriving at the 'fit' goes well beyond the ability of a candidate to assimilate a cultural philosophy or dress the part. This will provide your corporation with the best of human capital necessary to gain that competitive advantage in a global business arena. A number of corporations are attempting to shore up their competitive advantage through relationship building, and finding and retaining the adequate talent to facilitate the human capital needs of their organization. Many companies have done this through adding amenities to their organization like health spas, bonus programs, and other incentive plans that aim at maintaining a great cooperative working relationship between management and employees. This relational activity is to be applauded, and a positive cultural environment can lead to better performance and productivity, however, there are types of ineffective relationship building that can lead to a point of counter productivity when they transform themselves into relationships that supersede good business decisions. This is the syndrome that I refer to as to close to call relationships. Allow me to explain macro relationship or general relationship building in organizations that evolve into personalized relationships, and become more of a micro relationship or customized relationship where the employee develops an attitude of laissez faire. A culture of protectiveness fronts itself to the point of no matter how the organization is doing I will not be effected because management likes me to much. If another higher educated or more qualified employee comes onboard, it will not have an affect on my position because I am close with department management. When an organization or business has to step it up a notch to counteract competition in the marketplace these personal relations that stagnate business can be disastrous and the consequences self-destructive. As a point of reference look at businesses that umbrella themselves in bureaucratic nepotistic philosophies and culture where quality, performance, and educated employees are back seated in favor of the proverbial 'favorites'. To close for call comes into play when replacing qualified with un-qualified and high performers with mediocrity, all for the sake of friendships. To elaborate further, I am not condemning company performance rewards, health clubs, golf outings, or developing a great and productive relationship with the employees, I am attempting to project what I feel is unhealthy relationship building. Nepotism is a poison that through osmosis spreads through the entire company and kills productivity and performance.

Compensation planning must also be analyzed when searching for leaders to fill executive positions. During these tough economic times, many employers are attempting to get the best for less. Please do not use this approach because it will come back to get you. These executives will be the conduit of your strategic planning, and as soon as the economic storm passes, guess who will be leaving. Great talent is not easily replaced nor the strategies and initiatives of your company that will go with them. Talk about transparency. You will not only lose talent, but a great piece of your core competency mosaic. We have discussed at length the process for hiring adequate human capital to successfully run the turbines of your corporate engine, however, in the present corporate culture there is tremendous turnover in the C Suite that can send business reeling. Who will replace your top executives throughout the various departments as they look for other horizons and opportunities to pursue? Decisions to exit can happen overnight leaving your search teams scrambling and your corporate fabric unraveling.

I cannot insist enough on having a strategic plan in place for leadership succession and seamless business progression. There is the old adage that says if it is not broke do not fix it, yet no one thinks about preparing when it does brake.

Atrophy can set into a business when things are going smoothly. To explain this idea further, the thinking and strategic processes can slow down or come to a halt the smoother the operation is running. Your business must be on top of its game and always be prepared for any sudden changes or disruptions. Continued success can create a myopic vision if care is not taken. I am not being punitive about success; however, one must be careful not to take your eye off the ball. The loss of top talent can be devastating so there must be consistent preparation internally to build leaders and prepare for change.

6 TALENT DOWN THE DRAIN
The Great Resume Abyss

I can already feel the back draft from human resources departments concerning this very important issue, but I must insist on providing a blueprint regarding the great resume abyss. Human capital talent is the main resource and engine that powers the engine of business on an international basis. Empowering this talent can maintain the success of your business for many years through many storms, and will preserve and sustain the lifecycle of your business. The financial and profitability rewards from recognizing, securing, and empowering this human capital talent will benefit your business with the versatility and flexibility to realize a competitive advantage in your business arena. I am always bewildered when I conduct a human resources performance and metrics analysis on a variety of businesses, and the facts and findings point to poor performance levels at key positions within the company. The world possesses such a great talent basin on international levels that it was hard for me to believe that finding and capturing good talent would be a formidable task. Now I realize that many factors and variables go into a lapse in performance, as well as some smaller businesses cannot compete financially for the higher-level talent in the market, yet that is not what is always at issue. I have performed consulting analysis on job descriptions and strategic initiatives of businesses aligning them with the talent bank that the company has secured through the collection of resumes, and my hair would curl over the extraordinary amount of talent that is left untapped in the resume abyss for whatever reason. As stated in one of my earlier chapters, the 'fit' can keep your company unfit for duty and performance. For the system to run effectively, the organization must communicate the strategic plan to all members of the human resources team from associates to human resources managers and directors. I want to expand on a few of my findings in this very critical area of identifying, acquiring, and placement of the talent sitting in your resume abyss. To begin with, does your recruiting team know what the company is specifically looking for? Please remember, keep open communication. Is the right fit, that of your management team or just the flavor of the week for your recruiting team to decide on? I do not mean to be offensive or robust in my dialogue, however, the fit can be determined in many ways, but they may not always point to performance capabilities and business strategies that will keep your company effective and competitive for the long run. Just some recruiting nuances that I heard from recruiters in the field on conducting the proper fit analysis. This individual is a great party person, is comical, and is easy on the eyes. I hope you are listening all you CEO's, CFO's, Human Resources Managers, and Directors, as well as staff and line managers because this type of fit for duty may be the very catalyst for your negative ROI. The perfect fit should be a candidate who is aligned with the purpose and vision of the company.

The changes in workforce culture and the consistent challenge of a global economic business platform makes it imperative that recruitment of talent to meet and exceed these challenges be placed at the highest priority of your strategic planning. There is not one exact blueprint that empowers a business to succeed in this quest. Due to the economic shifts, strategic changes, and cultural philosophies all continue to change at a moments notice. What appeared to be in vogue yesterday has already been outdated in a 24-hour period. Your business and recruitment must keep their finger on the pulse of the business environment constantly to envision those changes as well as defining, locating, and acquiring new pools of talent on an international level. An open and continuous line of communication between multi functional departments must be the continuum for strategic success and talent acquisition. Communication must be infectious to the degree that permeates from the boardroom to every department below the C Suite. Position descriptions must be constructed with every strategic and business plan involved as well as expectations for emotional intelligence factors and leadership capabilities. This will empower your business to meet and exceed the continuous changes in the business climate, and obtain a forward vision to gain a competitive advantage in your business arena. In the current business market, I consistently see companies retooling, reinventing, and socially and culturally rethinking the environment of the business. This is all great, on the other hand, the acquired talent and position descriptions are not fitting into the plan. It is like trying to squeeze a size 9 business plan into a size 8 talent poll if you do not mind the metaphor. The plasma of the company is your acquired talent and it does not stop there. The human capital that you acquire must be empowered and developed to become leaders and developers of the framework of your business. When providing employees with the opportunity to grow their careers and to be contributors to the overall success, they will continue to strive to enhance your business and to view themselves as owner operators as opposed to just a spoke in the wheel.

The resume abyss that I mentioned in this chapter, although a vital technological tool, can be detrimental to the recognition of great talent if not set up correctly. I am not only referring to the technological architecture and the software programming involved, I am speaking of the artificial intelligence that goes into this as well as the keyword search. What are the processes that go into your keyword search? Are they set with the overall corporate strategy, or does one size fit all? Does the C suite get involved at any time with the human resources executives to make sure that the hiring processes are in alignment with the strategic vision of the company? In the technological environs of the great resume machine that I call search and seizure in the cyber sphere, there needs to be a carefully analyzed process of harnessing the talent in this giant black hole outside of a keyword search. Does this adequately spot check talent or provide the link for the talent to match your corporate strategy? I realize that with the massive amounts of resumes coming in there needs to be a systemic approach to separating the wheat from the chaff. There needs to be a collaborative effort with your human resources management and recruitment team in conjunction with your strategic objectives to define the proper information and identifying factors of spot-checking talent. The mistake happens when a one size fits all approach is applied to all positions that you are looking to fill. Finalizing my thoughts on this procedure could be summed up by stating that the keywords must be carefully crafted with tremendous thought and insight to acquire true talent. I also would advise spot-checking not only words but also entire resumes. As tedious as this may seem, it is better then letting real talent go down the drain, or should I say into the black hole.

7 THE SCIENCE OF SELECTION
The Situational Interview

Human Resources, the curtain has just came up, and you and your staff are the stars of the interviewing drama about to unfold, but before jumping into the interviewing script you have plenty of work to do prior to that major interview or orientation. This is not a stand-alone effort. The strategic objectives of each department that you are hiring for must be scripted into the behavioral interview process to ensure the best selection is made for each position. Now let us piece the behavioral interviewing process together to create a beautiful tapestry of alignment between strategic planning and employee selection. The interviewer should have three documents in preparation for the interview, the job description, the lists of strategic objectives, and the prepared behavioral interviewing questions aligned with these strategies. These questions must be open-ended, and must have the applicant respond to real life situations that coincide with the performance expectations and desired outlines of the duties and responsibilities of the department.

The intensity and length of the interview process must be determined by the level of the position for which you are hiring. The behavioral interview process should consist of note taking as well as the observation of the candidate's bodily movements and gestures. The lack of eye contact, incomplete sentences, hand gestures, and clock watching during the interview can convey as much information regarding the candidate as the responses to the intense questioning.

Communication skills, leadership abilities, and critical thinking are all the attributes that the interviewer needs to glean as they continue to assess the qualities of the candidate they are interviewing for the pre-planning stages of these interviews. The length of the interview as well as the space between each interview must be given careful attention. These interviews cannot and should not be rushed, and after the interview is completed, the interviewer should prepare a concise report on the leadership abilities, communication skills, confidence, and to compare the candidate's responses to the job description and strategic objectives of the company. Is this a tedious process? Emphatically, I say yes. Can your company afford not to utilize this process? Emphatically, I say no.

The budgetary dollars spent on training and development, employee selection and retention, and organizational development is staggering. Consistent turnover and employee replacement can immediately put your human resources budget in the red. That is why it is necessary to hire the right employee the first time. Consistently utilizing the procedures that I have exacted will not only assist your business with the right hire but will also provide you with the leadership that will assist your business with the proper leadership and human capital needed to benchmark your company, and increase your competitive advantage.

As I previously mentioned, the human resources department provides the rich plasma that is the nourishment of your organization. During the behavioral interview process there must be a composite analysis of the applicant, as well as the position to be filled. What do I mean? Well, you need to dissect all the vital components of the job description, the strategic initiatives of the business, the department that you are hiring for, and structure the interview accordingly. This can be facilitated by designing your questions in conjunction with the position that you are attempting to fill. Does this position require multi-tasking, a high level of emotional and intellectual intelligence, as well as leadership and critical thinking skills? Customizing your questions to fit the position will assist you in drilling down into the applicant in order to glean the information needed for the selection process. Let us examine this process further. Looking back at chapter two, I defined building performance as a structure where everyone from the C suite down needs to be involved in the plan. Primarily, I discussed that your organization needs to review and preview in order to know and beat your competition. You can accomplish this by doing a SWOT analysis (strengths, weaknesses, opportunities, and threats) of your organization, and then discussing and ascertaining your strategic and objective initiatives. When conducted thoroughly and with precision you will be able to establish the strategies to gain the competitive edge in your business arena. This is the groundwork for establishing the job descriptions and job redesigning, which you are utilizing to fill your positions. It is vital that the human resources department establish the functional and cognitive requirements for the position to format these strategies. I have discussed the cognitive requirements to facilitate the position; however, there are emotional qualifications that must be considered. In the hiring market today, EI (Emotional Intelligence) is being studied by the best business schools in the world as a vital component in the behavioral interview process. Cognitive skills as well as book and theory smarts are important, however, the emotional intelligence levels of a candidate are essential in situational management, as well as change management situations. Emotional intelligence is also very important in proper decision making and managing under stressful situations. Great leaders on the battlefield and in business possessed these qualities, and their importance cannot be diminished. Therefore, in the construction process of your behavioral interview, the structure must be set up in accordance with the strategic initiatives meeting the job description, the functional requirements reflecting the job description, and the cognitive, educational, and emotional intelligence level of each candidate meeting the requirements of this entire strategic process. Once the entire behavioral interview process is conducted in this format, you are looking at a win win situation. In the current international pool of applicants, the behavioral interview process has evolved. The current business model is one of globalization in the marketplace and diversity in the workforce. This is a hybrid that needs to be strategically pieced together to bring about the best of overall organizational effectiveness.

8 CHOOSE RIGHT THE FIRST TIME
Employee Selection

Once while visiting a retail business during the busy Christmas season, I encountered a manager nervously talking to a front-end supervisor. In his desperation, with arms raised, and eyes bulging he shouted, 'bodies! I need bodies'! It was obvious that during the peak holiday season he was short staffed, and his statement was very reflective of most business hiring practices today. Just so there is a body at station A. B. C., it is full steam ahead. That is at least until the steam is depleted and so is the business.

Proper employee selection is the plasma that runs the business, and should be at the heart of every business regardless of the size. Employee selection and retention in a very diverse employee market garnishes the business arena with a very rich pool of candidates, however, this diversity can also place many challenges to your business in regards to cultural sensitivities, and talent blending in the workplace. With training and organizational development budgets under the scope of the CFO, it is crucial that consistent replacement and retraining does not become a part of your corporate culture. You must implement an adept and thorough interview process regardless of what level of employee you are hiring. From the receptionist to the file clerk, from executive staff to line managers, and physical plant operations personnel included, the behavioral interview process must be put into effect to produce the best talent that would put the exclamation point at the end of your mission statement. You must view your business as an engine that must fire on all cylinders to be effective or stalling and hesitation will replace productivity and accuracy. Do not feel dejected if your business has not taken employee selection this seriously, you are part of a very large group, however, it is never too late to do an about face. You need to consider employee selection as part of the objective and strategic planning of your business. The branding, benchmarking, and competitive advantage processes of your company need to begin with the human capital to get you where you want to be. I was interviewing a Human Resources Manager at a manufacturing plant who informed me that it cost his budget $3000.00 per employee to train. Now this was a small to mid-size company, can you imagine the training costs involved in a fortune 500 concern? Employee retention is necessary in this competitive business market, and the cost of choosing incorrectly and losing an employee is staggering to the budget if this pattern persists. Sharp shooting behavioral techniques must be practiced and customized to each job description, in order to follow the strategic compass set forth in the company boardroom. These techniques must test the emotional intelligence level of each applicant, as well as, presenting real life critical thinking situations and how the applicant would apply them to each situation. Businesses must stay away from the mentality of quantitative hiring processes, where quantity replaces quality. That is great if you are just looking to staff bodies to make the proverbial widget on the assembly line, but let us think about that for a moment. If that widget is your product and the assembly lines your road to business success, you will still need responsible employees to meet your strategic expectations. Even in the most mundane of business operations, you need to have responsible creative and emotionally intellectual employees to produce the desired results. I want to emphasize again the necessity to staff your human resources department with employees who are totally on board with the strategic initiatives, and forward thinking processes of your company. I would be remiss not to revisit this very important component and vital link of your business success. Recently, I attended a church function where the priest was relating the context and message of his homily to the anatomy of the human heart muscle. He was stating emphatically the importance of this small but vital muscle that supplies and pumps the blood to the various organs in the body. This muscle, which is roughly two pounds, has the duty to supply and nourish all the vital components of the body, to ensure their capacity to work effectively and to keep the mind thinking and the body working as a fine tuned machine. I thought about this homily after leaving the church that day, and while not attempting to diminish the spiritual context of the message, I thought that there was also a connection in this analogy to the business world. I drew a comparison of this small but vital heart muscle to the human resources department of a corporation or business. I am not attempting to lay claim that the Human Resources department is a small component on the corporate grid, however, it is one of many components that make up the organization. The Human Resources Department plays a most vital role in supplying rich human capital to the various departments that is necessary for the life of the company. Although the heart continues to supply blood to the organs in the body in order to sustain, the quality of this blood must be in top shape in order to facilitate and nourish the ongoing work of the body. This is the duty of the human resources department, to continue to supply a rich quality of human capital to all the vital departments of the corporation to continue a high level of performance. This quality workmanship will be your core competency, prolong the longevity of your business, and provide value added vitality in your competitive business arena. When I was a youth in elementary school, I was taught to make sure that my work was worthy of placing my name on it. At times, being in a rushed position to turn in my work, my grade would reflect the importance of this statement. I was ultimately shamed by what I turned in with my name on it. This advice by my teachers has followed me throughout my career, and especially as a consultant. When I develop programs for hiring and staffing managers, as well as recruiters, I always hammer home the point that the employees you hire are like putting your name on your work. Although in this sense, this is the company name and image to their customers, clients, and suppliers. The star of the company will rise and fall not only by the decisions they make, but also by the employees they hire. I am not a firm believer in micro managing, however, it is imperative that executives and business owners maintain a concise metrics of all departments especially in the human resources area, not as big brother watching, but as a means to audit and troubleshoot problems that can be lethal to the lifecycle of your business.

9 GOLDEN FLEECE OF YOUR STRATEGY
Training and Development

Training and Development is one of the most vital areas of your organization, and at the same time, the most underrated area of your organization. Now before you are ready to start hurling your major disagreement litanies at me, let me emphasize my points. How many times have you needed to twist the arms of your management team to attend a training seminar unless the location of the training is at a resort with blue water, great scenery, and golden sunshine? This is not an attempt to be facetious, although this is a very cold reality about the corporate angst that's portrayed when the company schedules training seminars. I could write a book alone on the line of excuses that employees use for not attending these training seminars. Subsequently, when releasing the double-edged sword memo with the fiery word of mandatory carefully placed at the heading, the process of dragging in the team kicking and screaming now takes place. I never could perceive the reason for avoiding this process like the black plague, when it is the most important process for extending the play of your corporate lifecycle. A challenge that can be problematic is coordinating the employee-training program to meet the strategic goals of the company if not assessed and analyzed proficiently. I will begin to identify the procedural steps that you need to facilitate to properly conduct and develop a training and development program that will enhance the development and performance levels of your management and employees to gain the golden fleece of your competitive advantage.

Let us face reality all companies will face moments of inertia unless some outside force stimulates a reaction to your normal course of business. This outside force will produce either a knee jerk reaction or a reactive reflexive response. In the current economic crisis where competitive advantage is not an elective but a requirement, reactionary responses will not be the answer to the business market. You may remark, we have a strategy to compete, but is your strategy just a bigger shadow to what your competition is already offering in the market. Stimulation to new and more inventive ideas and better processes of bringing these all together is required to extend your lifecycle, extend the play, and capture the prize called success. Strategy is the forerunner, the prime mover of innovative success in personal and business life, as well as the stimulus for the proper construction of a training and development program. You need to envision the training and development program as a quilt with strategy as the common thread running through the entire fabric. The Achilles Heel in this entire process will be to maintain the status quo, which is an attempt to just to keep up with the competition, or to strengthen the ordinary. Your strategy in the business market especially the current business market is not to revitalize the ordinary, but to reinvent the ordinary and reenergize with innovation the offerings of products and/or services. You must develop your strategy and direction from auditing the competitive internal and external pulse of your business competition. You need to know their logistics and direction in order not to pursue them, but to gain the higher ground of innovation, technology, and product/service development. Training and Development must be a strategically crafted program that will coordinate the strategy and vision of your company with the talent of your human capital. The training and development program must be coordinated to elevate the performance of your human capital to meet and exceed the vision of your strategy. All this may sound very pedestrian, as I will demonstrate. Developing the training and development program is a consistent strategy of its own and not just something that you wing on a moments notice.

In order to develop a program properly there are appropriate steps to take to ensure that your program will meet the goals that you are trying to accomplish. For starters, their needs to be a strategic transparency within the corporate grid to ensure that all departments ascertain the short and long-term goals of the company. In the corporate business arena, all hands on deck need to know not only where the company is going, but also what is their place and role in this giant aggregate system. This is the genesis of training and development, and needs to be the road map of your training plan. During the Revolutionary War at the Battle of Bunker Hill, or Breed's Hill, at the most intense part of the conflict, a Continental General was heard to shout, "Don't shoot until you see the white's of their eye's". This was great advice from a strategic military perspective, however, in the business arena there are several reasons why a company decides to invest in a training and development program. The first reason for the investment is to provide the employees with the skills to adapt to a new technology, or to fine-tune their basic job duty requirements. Secondarily, training may be a reactionary, or knee jerk response to a competitor gaining ground on your market share, and you are attempting a different response to off set this business set back. While all of this is fine, training needs to be more organic and growth stimulated, not a reactionary tool, but one of an innovative plan to surpass the competition. Training programs require much thought work, critical analysis, interdepartmental cohesiveness, and transparency within the organization. The organizational strategy must flow like osmosis through the entire organization to all hands on deck, in order for the staff to know the purpose, vision, and reasoning behind the training. One may ask why this must take place in order to have an effective training program. At the beginning of this chapter, I stated that getting employees and managers to participate effectively in a training program is a tedious venture within itself. Knowing the purpose and vision of this mission and training, as well as their role in the overall plan, stimulates a culture of inclusion and importance within this organizational development planning. In the critical analysis phase of planning your training program, C level management as well as staff and line management must gather information on the market competition, and the entire competitive business arena utilizing cross functional teams from Marketing, IT, Human Resources and Finance to build your strategy and construct the road that you want to travel on. When you start this analysis phase, you are gathering information from many sources, however, when processing all this information you will need to adequately stimulate a critical analysis and arrive at the right solution for development of the training program. Through this analysis phase, you will determine the correct problem in your organization that needs to be resolved if that is why you are designing this training program. You may be designing this training program because you have purchased or developed a new technology that will profit your corporation with a huge competitive advantage, and your human capital needs to be brought up to speed in this process. I like to call this training evolutionary training since you are messaging the intellect and being organic and growing new ideas that will provide market and new market penetration.

Ok, let the training design begin. You already know why there is a need for training, and what you need to achieve. Now how do we roll this out? First, you need to meet with the Finance Department to determine your budget for this entire process, and oh yes, training takes money, and can you feel the C level quaking already? There may be a mentality of budget by the door and training out the window, however, when the Finance and Budget departments provide you with the numbers, then you will able to identify the length and breadth of your program. You will ascertain how many employees to invite, will this training be in-house, or through a professional consulting firm, and what should be the duration of the training program. If your organization possesses the expertise in the particular area that you are training for, then you can utilize that human capital to provide the knowledge transfer of information to train and develop your employee base. This can provide a tremendous cost savings to your business or organization. Subsequently, if you need to utilize the services of a professional consulting firm, you will need to do some extensive homework. Primarily, you need to research the firm's background and the cost involved. Other factors to consider are references of former businesses that have utilized their services, and the efficiency and cost benefit analysis of their programs. If you choose to select a private consulting firm, you should invite them to your business to view a dry run of their program. You will need to have questions addressed such as how do they train a multi-cultural workforce where there may be language barriers, and are they equipped to facilitate hearing-impaired employees. Your organization will need to address these concerns to decide whether to go in house to facilitate the training as opposed to an outside vendor. Most importantly, if you take the route of a private training consultant this could be a very expensive endeavor that may require expenditures that may leave a good size hole in your budget. After performing your internal metrics audit and SWOT analysis which will assist you in pinpointing the problem and narrowing down problem areas that will require the training, you can take measures to control the financial strains on your training budget. You can streamline expenditures by inviting your main knowledge staff of employees to attend the training sessions instead of inviting the whole staff, which will dramatically cut back on cost per employee. You can then upstream the training through transfer of knowledge to other employees within the department. This will achieve the desired results at a cost savings on your training budget. The training sessions needs to be perpetually monitored on a daily basis to acquire the desired results. Your organization can achieve this by gathering feedback from the employees in the form of dialogue and response cards that they will need to complete at the end of each session highlighting what they gained from the sessions and its effectiveness. These response cards are a very important tool in gathering information and feedback, in order to make necessary adjustments to the program. Remember, even if you have a private consultant performing the training, you need to take ownership of the program to initiate the desired outcomes. At all times within the training program, you must delegate order and professionalism to achieve the results. Supervision of this program is necessary in order to prevent noise pollution such as talking out during training, superfluous joking, and tardiness. These elements will negate the entire purpose of the training sessions for those who are interested in learning and benefiting from the program. Organizational effectiveness is the primary driver of this training and development program, and without being redundant, it must be tailored to extend the play and vitality of your company or business. A training program should never be conceived as a means of tailgating the competition as they press forward, and you attempt to keep up as a reaction to their progress. Your training program must be the learning class and the instructional podium for your human capital to learn as you develop new products and services, as well as new technologies to expand your market footprint and benchmark your business. Training should never be an exercise in futility, and consistently playing catch up ball with the competition as a catalyst for developing a training program is swimming against the current. Research and development must continuously be brainstorming for new products and services, and your IT unit must be searching for innovative technological advancements to compliment increased production methods, and fluidity in delivery of goods and services. With these processes in mind let the transfer of knowledge begin by developing the best training and development programs utilizing your best asset, your human capital.

10 METRICS FOR SUCCESS
Auditing the Functionality of Departments

Every architect has a blueprint for the project that he/she is developing, just like the strategic planning that is conceived and developed to compliment the goals and initiatives of the business. You cannot change what you cannot measure. In order to successfully evaluate, monitor, and gage the level of performance of each department and functional unit of your business, a metrics model must be designed and detailed to properly provide the information necessary for management to make the proper decisions in carrying out the strategic goals and initiatives of the company.

The metrics grid must be strategically designed inclusive of every position within every department, and a numeric value must be associated with each position according to the importance level of the job. An example of a numeric metrics grid would be as follows: Receptionist position--requirements of position-- You may rate the expectations of this position on a level of 1-5, Computer Skills--rate 1-5 according to competence level on utilizing software programs, Customer Service Skills--rate 1-5 according to phone answering skills, communication skills, and multi-tasking abilities. This is just a brief example of breaking down each position according to the position description, and placing a numeric value on each job function according to the importance of each function. This measuring and evaluating will enable management to measure and gage the problem areas as well as to define the areas where performance is excelling. Other positions my have to be rated higher in the metrics grid according to the level of the position and the multitude of functions within the description. One caveat that I would expect of management is never to under evaluate any position, and to consider all positions as a major part of the corporate strategic planning. The face of the corporation is the front desk receptionist who greets all external and internal customers. He/she is the reflection of the mission statement, and the first person that portrays the image of the company.

In a Japanese garden where waterfalls abound, the rocks and formations that form the falls and topography generally rise in a motion as if going from earth to heaven. I mention this in a perspective that there is a connection going back and forth from above to below, and from below to above, each one feeds off the other. This is the strategic planning and metrics for your company. Planning, communication, involvement, monitoring, evaluating, measuring, and appraisal must flow like plasma through all facets of the corporation in order for the strategic plans and goals to be measured and standards met. This is the embodiment of performance for competitive advantage. I would be remiss if I did not state the fact that metrics is a continuous process, and is not a once in the while process. Business and competition is changing constantly, and at times your business model must be like a Chameleon. We use this metaphor in life to designate a person that changes from one thing to another, or one pretending to be something that they are not. This is not the context in which I am using the word Chameleon. I am using this word in the sense the you will need to change, adapt, and grow with your customers exponentially to meet and exceed their expectations. The Chameleon at times changes colors constantly, and with quite a surprise, not for the use of camouflage purposes. It does this to make itself more attractive to potential mates in their daily world. Is this not what businesses must do especially in a down economy to make itself attractive to customers? It must be at times all things to all people and color themselves with the current tastes and needs of society. These changes in the daily business arena must consistently be the driver that stimulates the analysis needed to accurately define and refine the metrics of each department of your business concern. Your metrics analysis must be done at every level with every department. I consider this like tracing a bad wire that is not making contact properly. You cannot just check one wire to find the fault; sometimes several wires are responsible for the lack of adequate current or no current at all. It would be great if your business model was one big circuit that you can change or reset when it struggles or shortens out, however, it is many circuits in the form of human capital and efficiency that needs to be traced and checked, and at times reset with training and consistent quality improvement. Remember always that your procedures need to be measurable in order to determine if they have met standards.

11 THE PULSE OF BUSINESS
Monitoring and Evaluation

As I mentioned in chapter four relating to hiring right the first time, let me now speak to you concerning the follow-up process after the employee selection has been made. All business is organic, it continues to grow or shrink governed by the successes or failures of the strategic planning and implementation of your business leadership. The same star must guide all corporate governance and management in order to benchmark your company as the best in your competitive arena. Leadership and development just does not happen, it is a process of consistent monitoring and evaluation, coaching and praising, correcting and modifying, as well as revising and retooling. Yes, there certainly is a process, but once again, it starts at the very beginning where the blueprint and the strategic objectives are put into place. This is the GPS for your business. There is a concise process of interior monitoring and exterior analysis. Now please do not panic and say, 'Another Process'! You will see that this is actually a 360-degree process with continuous motion, and your management and employee base are the gravitational pull that keeps this sphere in balance.

As your company maps these procedures and practices into the daily operations of the company, it is almost as if they were osmotically transmitted through the entire organization. Let us first talk about the interview monitoring process. Your company has a strategy plan for competitive advantage, and the best employees are being hired to carry out this plan of attack. Easy, right? Well, yes, but like the sales pitch, wait, there is more. These sharp shooters of the industry that you hire can grow stale through mundane and redundant operational procedures. Management must maintain an open line of communication, conveying informational updates to the staff and employees in order to keep everyone on the same page. This will assist in making corrections or modifications to the daily procedures. If strategic planning changes are made from upper management, and neglectfully not communicated to subordinate management, this will be a plan to fail. Monitoring and evaluating must be done on a macro-organizational level to secure your competitive advantage and secure your benchmark in the business arena. For a brief moment let your imagination conceptualize this monitoring and evaluation process as compared to an automotive technician trouble shooting and performing a diagnostic analysis on the engine of your vehicle. Every component and every running part of that engine must be monitored, evaluated, and analyzed before a clear and concise diagnosis can be properly determined to effectively solve the problem and have the engine fine-tuned again. Just like this engine, the organization must be monitored, evaluated, and analyzed in order to maintain a fine-tuned well performing organizational structure. Micro managing may send cringes up the spine of managers and employees alike; however, at times this situational management style may be needed to make changes during a critical evaluating and monitoring process.

For the purpose of being concise and detailed, let us examine the stages of monitoring, evaluating, and mentoring one at a time, and apply the necessary philosophies and artisanship to each one. Within the organization, to identify factors adequately that may positively or negatively affect the strategic initiatives and goals of the organization we must first begin with the monitoring process. You may ask, why are we looking at the positive factors, are they not a self-sustaining part of the overall performance? Well, yes, though they may be an interchangeable component of the organization, they may be utilized at another critical mass juncture of the performance plan, or provide great feedback on streamlining or improving operational procedures. This monitoring of the operational procedures is an essential component of improving and revitalizing the day-to-day operations of the company. This must be considered as a best practice method in order to secure a high performing degree of reliability and quality standards when diagramming your strategic initiatives on the whiteboard before your executives and staff management. Every vital component of the organization must be monitored from the human capital to the day-to-day operations and how they are being performed. Does this employee serve a better purpose here or in another area of operations? Could this operation be stream lined? Are they being performed at the highest level of efficiency? All these questions must be asked and evaluated for a results driven organization to be competitive. A metrics system must be designed and developed that establishes the standards and goals for each functional department of the organization, and take a monthly statistical analysis to compare results against the standards that were established with the strategic planning. These metrics will be a cross reference enabling management to define, refine, and solve problem areas before they spread like a virus through the organization. These metric results will now empower management with the analysis to evaluate each functional unit of operations, and develop a plan to effectively fix any problem areas. After the evaluation process, areas of the operations that fell below the standards met on the metrics chart must provide coaching and training methodologies to strengthen low performance clusters. While evaluating and monitoring, do not be stingy with the praise that should be rewarded to high performing areas of the operations. In some management circles, this is viewed as a negative effect on performance. They believe that rewarding employees with praise, results in a disconnect in the continuity of good performance. The assumption is that employees will take advantage of a reward or praise system from management. This may be the case with some employees, though in a healthy positive corporate culture this will be an added incentive for employees to be more productive and feel an inclusive part of the overall strategic goals and successes of the company. This is a fatal error that many companies make in the area of organizational development and training. I have seen corporations place employees in very vital roles without providing them with the proper training to effectively perform their job. The only training they are afforded is Q & A sessions with their colleagues in the department who may not even have the required experience in that position. I relate this to double teaming a receiver in a football game; someone is left in the open when this defense is used. Well, apply the same principle to the employee providing the assistance as his/her function is left wide open with no one there to continue the operation, and productivity stops. Imagine an employee doing this three or four times a day over a year, you do the math. What is more costly, the training or lost production? Repetition brings consistency, so remember the mantra; Monitor, Evaluate, Coach, and Praise.

12 THE ORGANIC CORPORATION
Change or Die!

For a company to remain a top performer and retain a successful competitive advantage, organic growth is necessary. In relationship to Darwin's theory of natural selection where plants, animals, and even whole civilizations existed or died off according to their adaptability to changes in the environment, the 21st century organization must be flexible and adaptable to real time consistent change or it will also die off. Technically, the theory of natural selection should be an ever-present philosophical model transcending into the objective and strategic initiatives of your business or corporation. Survival of the fittest is the basic lifecycle of the business world, and your business model must be adaptive to the consistent changes in the marketplace. Keeping your finger on the pulse of the market, focusing on your customer's needs, and finding the one best way to do this better then your competition, is the challenge that must be micro managed and accomplished on a daily basis.

Product design and marketing are only the beginning of competitive advantage. One must continue to keep their eye on the ever-changing innovations in technology in order to enhance their product sets and expand the lifecycle of old products, while submitting to the desires of the populous and bringing new and innovative products to market. This consistent progress must be your branding, your signature service, in order to secure your place as a leader in your particular industry. Your business must be able to retool, reinvent, and even dare to enter new and enticing markets to be competitive; re-visioning, now here is an interesting concept. Maybe the widgets that were your cash cow for years are no longer the flavor of the week. Well, now it is time to see what the market demands and in what direction they are heading. Ok, where does this re-visioning need to start? The CEO, CFO, CIO, board of directors and management call a major boardroom meeting to discuss the decline in sales. Discussions of shifts in market trends, and bewilderment as to why the mission statement they presented to customers, stake holders, and stockholders reflecting a tremendous outline of success and responsibility is becoming more fiction then fact.

Let us start to dissect the principle issues of this boardroom melodrama. Generally, human nature voluntarily agrees to utilize the parasympathetic part of the Autonomic Nervous System. This is the part of our structure where we want to relax, chill out, and enjoy a little euphoria. We select this process and even plan for it. There is nothing wrong with this, and I believe that our workforce needs to do a little more of this to enhance creativity and productivity. When we are unexpectedly hit by a rogue wave or placed in a perilous position, this is when the sympathetic system kicks in and allows us either to fight or flight. One example would be walking into a dark room and having someone jump out at you. Will we challenge the person or run and hide. The Sympathetic System is generally used, corporately speaking, when situations such as the ones in our boardroom discussion above take place. What happened? When did this happen? Why did this happen? Why were we caught off guard? These events should have been monitored instead of attempting to facilitate them by way of a knee jerk reaction. Being pro active in your company through the monitoring, evaluating, coaching, praise (remember these), and communicating with Research and Development, Training and Development, and micro managing the market trends with a keen sense of customer demands and needs will help to curtail these what happened boardroom discussions. This system will empower and enable you to protect against those situations that jump out at you unexpectedly in the dark that cause you to react in varied ways. Let us start to be pro active instead of reactive. Your preemptive fight may be the catalyst of your competition to take the reactive flight. The organic business world calls on us daily to make very visionary decisions. Major discussions in the boardroom are consisting of entry into Europe, Far East, Middle East, and Third World Country markets to remain competitive and extend the play of their corporate lifecycle. This is where the think tank of the organization has to sit down and readily examine and analyze the SWOT analysis of their business climate to make this determination. Any corporation who wants to remain successful must continue to cultivate new innovation and technology, exploring new and emerging markets to do business, and new product sets to meet the ever-changing needs and demands of their customers.

To secure your competitive advantage, you must continue to secure your intellectual property. I simply do not mean to narrow this down to software and programming, in addition you need to include your greatest asset of intelligence, which is your human capital. This can be done by developing a corporate culture of inclusiveness, empowerment, and promoting the leadership capabilities of your employees. Retaining top employees and progressive talent management continues to enhance the creative culture of your business, which leads to innovation and organic strategic accomplishment. Employers must also be very competitive in the areas of compensation and benefit packages for talent retention. Creativity must be a constant process to survive in the organic competitive business market. Management must continue to monitor the pulse of product lines to determine slow growth products that need divested or changed to be market competitive. Analysis must be done to insure proper allocation of costly limited production resources to increase ROI and present a healthy cash flow for corporate stakeholders and stockholders. To remain competitive in the organic marketplace you will need to reinvent the wheel. Even tire manufactures have found better and more innovative ways to enhance the basic tire molds to meet the ever-changing needs of the marketplace. I think, therefore I grow, must be your corporate mantra. For a business or corporation to grow and develop in an organic thriving environment, you must have leaders who are visionary and tactful internally and externally throughout the company. Consistent changes in the marketplace, and real time response to consumer needs, must be continuously monitored and adapted to your internal environment, as well as your corporate culture and human capital. Your internal culture and employees need to be committed, flexible, and adaptable to changing technologies and knowledge advancements in crucial business segments and global grids. Economies are changing invariably throughout the global spectrum, and as these changes are taking place, your leadership team must be on the alert for competitive advantage opportunities and roadblocks that need to be proactively challenged. Your strategy to be an organic and thriving organization must be your awareness of these changes and opportunities and collaborate with your internal environment.

13 FIVE P'S OF MARKETING FOR PERFORMANCE

From the days of studying marketing in undergraduate school, we had the four P's of marketing drummed into our craniums. Like a mantra, we repeated: Product, Place, Promotion, and Price. Just when you think you have them remembered, here I go giving you a fifth one to remember, Performance. This is what I mean by reinventing the wheel, and thinking outside the proverbial box. You may ask why performance? Without an effective plan for performance, the other four can be cancelled out. Think of it in this fashion. You plan to attend a Broadway show that has been heavily promoted, from the advertising to the price of the tickets. Upon finally attending this show, the product, place, price, and promotion are no longer thought of just the performance. If the performers do not deliver up to the expectations of the hype and marketing, the show will be a disaster. I do not mean to trivialize the four P's of Marketing; however, without performance it voids the other four.

To set the stage for your marketing strategy many areas of thought have to be analyzed, calculated, and set into action in order to follow the strategic goals and initiatives of your company as well as the financial projections desired. The business analysts and business development specialists have to set a plan into action that will determine the sweet spots in the market that they need to penetrate. Your company may entertain the possibility of entering into Emerging Markets or Pacific Rim countries, as well as the Middle East to Far East opportunities that demonstrate fertile ground. These decisions require the minds of many departments such as Finance and Accounting, Human Resources, Training and Development, and Research and Development. To start with, your company will have to determine how to finance International Markets. Determinations must be made on how to facilitate the fluctuations in currency with a strong or weak dollar. Will hedging of currencies be a necessity in a volatile economy or will a direct investment in building a plant in your target country be a consideration? If you direct invest, and utilize the financial resources from abroad to finance your domestic operations back home, what decisions will you make to offset a declining domestic currency? From a Human Resources perspective, how will your staffing needs be facilitated in International Markets? Will you utilize expatriate staffing or train and develop nationals in the host country? What cultural barriers will need to be addressed as far as religion, customs, language, and cultural observances? Research and Development also needs to be addressed as far as products and services being rendered in International Markets. Do these products and services conflict with the culture of the country? The naming and branding of the product should be researched to make sure that the words used have a relative or desired meaning. Many products have sat on shelves in International Markets due to the fact that the very name of the product had an entirely different meaning internationally then it had domestically. A caveat of uncertainty must also be demonstrated in the governments of host countries. Do these countries have stabilized governments, are terrorism prevalent, are constant outside threats from other countries always on the horizon? These questions and many others must be brain stormed before reaching a consensus.

The concepts that I am detailing are not evolutionary in thought, though many businesses in International Markets have been caught off guard by not pre-addressing one or more of these issues. Internationally and domestically speaking, a constant eye of attention must be kept on the pulse of the market as far as customer demands and their ever-changing desire for new products and services. Remember, if your business does not supply or fulfill the needs, someone else will. I cannot state enough that the business arena is a living, breathing, organic unit that feeds off the appetites of the consumer. Business is a 24/7, 365 days a year operation that never sleeps, and if the driver at the wheel becomes lethargic or tired, off the road you go into the pit. Pricing is another issue that has a life of its' own. How do you want to establish the pricing model? Here are a few ideas to dwell on prior to jumping quickly to a decision. What are the complimentary goods in the industry or are you the sole provider of this good or service? What sets your product or service apart from the others in your target markets? Do you have the technology and production capabilities to meet the supply and demand in order to stabilize pricing and sell at a comfortable profit margin? Remember, if your business is the exclusive supplier of this product or service, and you market it in a tight narrow target market, you can set the price and set the market providing the per capita income is elastic in your target market. This is a luxury to a business and generally not the norm in an aggregate global supply chain of products and services. To reiterate my opening thoughts in this chapter, all the products, placing, pricing, promotion will be left behind, if the performance of carrying out these duties in a diligent and adept manner is missing from the equation.

One caveat that I always mention in my talks at business seminars and symposiums is the fact of transparency of products and core competencies to your competitive business arena. Companies that have established markets in countries such as China have released patent and product development information as the allowance of gaining access to this major market. This is the trade off to secure position in these markets. I also want to speak to the area of knowledge sharing. This is another process that has gained leverage in large foreign arenas as a means of allowing access to populous foreign markets where product saturation can produce multi million dollar sales results. These types of business dealings may produce instant gratification and a high level of monetary results, however, one only needs to examine the long-range results of these actions, and they can be catastrophic to the long-term security and profitability of your business. As a business leader, you must examine the depth of the pool before jumping in. Sharing of knowledge and product development is comparable to locking the door of your home but leaving the window open. I would advise against having these actions become a part of your marketing plan. You need to examine your cost of producing these goods as well as the labor costs involved in maintaining high quality human capital. The reasoning behind this is the fact that once your product development cycle has become transparent to these markets, they can be replicated and produced with lower cost labor, as well as substituted with a modified product of marginal quality at a lower price. Well, do the math. Your rainbow has just lost its' vibrant colors. I am not claiming that you should avoid these markets, however, you should examine the long-range effects before counting the short-term dollars.

14 IS YOUR CULTURE THE RIGHT FIT?
Organizational Effectiveness

Recently, while presenting a seminar to business managers, the topic came up concerning an appropriate corporate culture to run a successful business. I was pleasantly surprised at the responses that resonated throughout the class. One Operations Manager replied that at his company they have a very relaxed culture with such amenities as blue jean Friday's, and Wednesday company luncheons. Another young woman stated that at her company they get to enjoy water cooler Monday's, where they are allowed to discuss their weekends, and how they enjoyed them. She stated that management permitted this in order to eliminate the employees becoming social butterflies. I heard many other amenities being mentioned of a similar nature all guised under the title, 'this is our culture.' On my drive home after class, I reflected on the feedback regarding corporate culture, and realized that the one common thread that weaved through them all had nothing to do with performance. I feel compelled to elaborate on my thought to ensure the reader that in no way I am against having amenities as part of the workplace culture. I feel that employee interaction and casual Friday's are great in and of itself; however, there are more variables that go into an efficient corporate culture that I feel gets left unattended but necessary.

Let us first visit this idea of a corporate culture, which has taken on a whole culture of its own. We hear so much of this today when selling the company to employees and perspective applicants as a draw or enticement to win talent to the organization. I hear this so often in discussions with students who land their first job, as they go into a litany of amenities that the company offers only to witness a few months later that they have already left for better opportunities due to a lack of a learning environment or upward mobility opportunities. This is exactly the point that I would like to use as a driver for company executives and human resources executives. When you are branding your business, the strategies and goals that your company sets out to achieve in order to set the high water mark against the competition, must be primarily to set the culture of a learning and high performance environment. This is the culture that I have seen placed on the back burner, leaving the other stimulants at the engine that drives the human capital. In the human condition, we all have a desire to achieve the highest level of our potential. Organizational effectiveness feeds off the company's organizational behavior or culture like a predator, and once this is out of balance it presents catastrophic results. I have seen businesses promote the laissez faire attitude as a business culture in order to attract a wide base of applicants who enjoy working in a leisurely environment with very little structure in the job description. Now this environment may be a staple for your corporate culture; however, the caveat comes into play when this environment is more of a promotional technique for quantifying applicants, then one that does support the organizational goals. The short answer needs to be addressed in a simple fashion; what culture and organizational behavior will I need to implement to ascertain the best organizational effectiveness? In the business arena, there will never be a one-size fits all answer to this question, however, there is a workable equation that all begins with your strategy. How does your business define and benchmark itself against your competitive environment? Are you primarily in business to just keep up with the competition or possibly even be willing to tailgate the competition just as long as you maintain an average bottom line? With this business vision, you then would be an excellent fit for the laissez faire culture. This will at least provide you with a base of revolving door employees to staff your comfort culture. Am I being a little derisive? Well, yes and no. Some businesses will thrive on a relaxed culture, and in fact will need this in order to be successful in their particular arena. The point that I hope to drive across is that some businesses will implement this culture as an employment driver to keep up with socioeconomic trends regardless of the strategy and organizational goals that they hope to achieve. An old adage states you should never take your work home with you, conversely you also cannot attempt to evolve your work environment into your home. This square peg into the round hole syndrome is being driven by social trending, dual income households, and employment law legislation that are continuously striving to unite home life and work life experience. I am definitely in favor of presenting the best workplace environment for the employee base, however, the main strategy is to lead an environment where employees are engaged, empowered, and presented with a learning environment to do their jobs effectively and with high performance. This should be the birth child of every strategy in business, and the nucleus in which all other factors revolve around. There is a process for integrating performance into organizational effectiveness, and this is through intercultural communications and team building processes that will streamline operational procedures and strategic efficiency. Determining and facilitating the influential culture of your business is a forward thinking process designed to effectively promote the corporate lifecycle. Sustainability is the key to longevity and growth. Viewing a corporate culture that will promote organizational effectiveness entails a 360-degree checkup of coordinating the strategy with human capital and interfacing these two components into a successful and enterprising business. Well beyond the corporate gymnasium, flextime schedules, and casual Friday's there are other attributes that need to be implemented into the overall culture that are at times neglected. Employment empowerment, engagement, and value centered best business practices are not idealisms, they are philosophies that must be incorporated into the human capital stream. A corporation or business must define the strategy and then define the culture that fits the environment. Many companies make the fatal mistake of letting the culture define the strategy, and succumb to the many external pressures that society defines as a culture. Without a doubt, external factors such as societal changes, family needs, and flextime environments must be realized into your cultural checklist in order to preserve an employee work life balance, however, there is also a business culture that needs to be initiated in order to successfully preserve the lifecycle of your business. Business cultures must be reflective of the strategy and business model that you are attempting to brand. If your business is a very labor-intensive production facility, you may need to incorporate a culture of teamwork and continuous quality improvement as a model culture. Your business may be a highly confidential software industry where you need to consistently promote a culture of trust, confidentiality, and consistent research and development as a bulwark in your environment. These are often the forgotten segments of the cultural aspects, which also need defined in a business climate to meet the strategy. Combining these with the life balance segment cultural aspects of a business environment promotes longevity of the business and a great retention plan for your human capital base.

This very important game plan must be implemented into the hiring strategy of the human resources team when preparing a behavioral interviewing model to acquire the right talent to fit this aggregate strategy. The interviewing for organizational effectiveness to adequately meet and service the needs of the organization must fall within the perimeters of your work life balance culture and organizational effectiveness culture. As I stated, the human resources team is the supplier of the plasma that keeps the heart of the industry or business running by choosing and acquiring the right talent that will meet and exceed the demands of your business environment. The business world is an organic and evolving environment, and the C Suite executives and management must keep the human resources executives and team informed of business and cultural changes that tend to change on a daily basis to hire, train, and develop the right talent. This process delegates that there must be a continuous stream of good communication and information flowing through these departments, and that is another culture in and of itself.

Culture and organizational effectiveness must be organic and mutually inclusive and situational from a strategic point of view. One type of culture that worked in the past may no longer be a fit for the continuous change that is infectious in the current business environment. The present economic condition delegates that cultures and strategies from C-Level on down may need to be changed and rethought in order to navigate the unchartered waters of the new global business environment. Job descriptions, job requirements, management processes, and talent management will have to adapt to situational circumstances as they change daily or weekly to meet the ever-changing consumer needs and demands. A culture of laid back and regimented may have to reshape quickly and evolve into a culture of fast paced and ambiguous as employees may be called on to learn new jobs and technologies in a very demanding environment. As Darwin stated in his theory of evolution that only the fittest survive, this will also apply to human capital as businesses and corporations proactively and reactively shift policies and procedures to model their business. Human Resources will be placed in a very demanding culture as they redefine the talent management and hiring strategies that will need to be implemented. The Board of Directors and C Level executives will have to keep their finger on the pulse of business and economic climates in order to take proactive measures to make these cultural transitions less dramatic and intense, in order for the human capital base to be able to absorb and adapt to this new environment. Organizational effectiveness and culture, quilted together in the right format, can provide a beautiful mosaic and be the catalyst for business success and longevity. This culture needs to be the right fit for the corporate business environment in order for both to be effective. United they will stand, divided they will fall. Corporate executives and managers at times attempt to force fit external cultural trends into the daily operation activities of the company with the hopes of uniting in harmony a stimulating environment working in conjunction with operating procedures; this plan will certainly fail. Extending the play of your business will have to be a culture that has an appreciation for the humanistic needs and philosophies that are exposed in the current business arena.

To succeed in the current business market, promoting organizational effectiveness, and the training and development of staff to meet the continuous strategic changes that are daily taking place should and must be the front-runner. With the economy going into a reset mode, there is no more business as usual. Everyday processes need to be audited and rethought in accordance with the catalyst that is changing the current business models. Corporate cultures find a comfort zone in maintaining a period of flux, and comfort may no longer be the norm of the day.

Guaranteed, many business cultures will be changing, and there may be no recycled cultures as the business models take on change as they battle onward for sustained competitive advantage. Managers may plead their case that a one-size culture can fit all. This may be in an attempt to take the escape hatch from the agony of restructuring a culture to fit the current business model. Revisions of a culture can take a serious toll from a humanistic approach as new philosophies play tug of war with the psychological stimuli of the human capital.

15 GROWTH ON THE HORIZON
The Emerging Market Niche

From a global footprint perspective, it is necessary for businesses and corporations to redefine their borders and embrace logistically the possibilities of doing business in emerging market countries as a means of gaining market share and solidifying their competitive advantage. Markets often times require a tremendous amount of thought leadership and forward thinking to capture these opportunities and gain a footprint in this arena. From a leadership perspective, a business must approach these markets on a collaborative effort from the C suite through the Marketing, Human Capital, and Finance Departments. This will ensure that the strategic planning involved in this endeavor through osmosis will inebriate the entire corporation. Preparing to entertain these markets cannot be a knee jerk reaction, or a pie in the sky feeling. The cultural and philosophical idealism of your human capital from the CEO to the receptionist must acquire a mentality of competitive advantage through expansionism. This requires a learning and training cultural environment. Your company must study the language, culture, customs, and philosophies of the emerging country where you attempt to make a footprint. Your business model must be one of an international flavor, or you must be all cultures and philosophies on an international basis. A consistent thought leadership process must follow through a scientific methodology of reasoning. Wow, that sounds like work! If your organization approaches these emerging market ventures from a direct investment in that particular country, then your business model needs to develop a strategy from the ground level of the country where you are conducting business. Your business now needs to strategically put on the mask of that country, take adoption of their cultures and philosophies, and acquire a oneness with their people and customs, which are necessary steps to take in order to understand how you will have to function in that particular business environment. These are just the idealisms that you need to explore and understand in order to do business in an emerging market country. Understanding their product tastes and consumer needs is a completely different matter. When selling cars, manufacturing products, or transacting business of any kind in international and emerging markets, especially when conducting business as a direct investment, can be quite a daunting task.

You need to market and prepare your products and services according to the religious, ethical, and cultural philosophies of each country where you are conducting business. Onboarding human capital whether it comes from your own domestic resources or acquiring foreign capital from the country that you are doing business with must be treated and customized according to the laws and customs of that country. Your business must abide by the legal and ethnic customs to be successful in that arena and gain competitive advantage. The many other considerations that must be designed to be effective are the governmental and financial pieces such as currency considerations and government regulations. Is the government in this country stabilized? Is the currency consistent in value or volatile to market corrections and conditions? This definitely seems like a heavy commitment to take on in order to gain a competitive advantage and increase your business footprint, however, the profit and market share can be tremendous.

Conducting business with major European Markets is quite different from doing business with small emerging market niches. Geographically and topographically speaking there are other considerations to examine when determining what emerging countries to place your footprint. Unlike doing business in other European countries, which are developed in the areas of mass transit, roads and bridges, as well as waterways that make accessibility for raw materials, and distribution of goods and services more viable, emerging countries are challenged in these areas. The pockets of wealth that these countries can bring to a business are tremendous, in light of their needs that are many, due to the primitiveness of their culture and the lack of accessibility to these goods and services. That is the good part. The challenge of your business now is having the talented human capital to meet the challenges of facilitating the cultural barriers and philosophies of these countries, and defining the needs of a challenging and demanding topography where roads and access routes need to be constructed. Determining the needs and cultural acclimations of your goods and services as well as the ability to build production facilities, and have distribution centers are issues that seem relatively common sense, yet they have been the ignored and forgotten premise of performance planning that has been the financial demise of many businesses.

The fit for this venture is strictly a talented pool of human capital who can deliver thought leadership, forward thinking, and big picture perceptual analysis. Spare no expense in this venture when considering the proper talent fit as the ROI can produce excellent results. George Washington understood well the discipline and empowerment that was needed to guide his troops to a successful campaign. He micro-managed each troop and every situation. He was a tough disciplinarian who only desired soldiers who could be taught, trained, and had the potential for leading others in battle if the challenge came up. He realized in the fog of the battle theatre, the war could scatter the troops in many a direction out of their normal formation and unit. Leadership and discipline were a necessary combination for a successful campaign, and this applies to the fit in the business theatre today. Micro managing each unit in every department can be a very counter-productive method of performance, although at times it may be required in situational management processes. With a proper interviewing model and selection process, disciplined employees and leaders can be obtained to take your business where it needs to be. When bodies are selected in place of talent just to perform a particular job function this makes micro managing an important factor of production, and one that unites managers and supervisors.

Let us once again revisit George Washington at Valley Forge. He did not have the advantage of high profile interviewers, and a human resources staff of qualified professionals to assist in the selection process of his troops. He had to take what he had, and that is where his leadership abilities rose to the occasion. Where George Washington did have an advantage, was that he was blessed with patriot troops who had a desire, a purpose, and unification of discipline. These qualities were reinforced with leadership that was respected and believed in. Once management participates in what they teach, these qualities are easy to absorb by your subordinates. When employees are empowered and encouraged to bring the best of their talents to the strategic planning, they feel a sense of ownership and pride in their mission. Remember, in previous chapters I stated that performance begins at the reception desk, and to mitigate any talent or position in the strategic planning could be lethal to your business. Empowering each employee at every position, as well as bringing out their best talent and qualities is an ability that every manager should have.

In the business arena, everyday can be a Valley Forge, and we all need a George Washington. The old adage always states that true leaders are born not made, however, the other part of that equation is that consistent, and progressive development still needs to be implemented and maintained throughout their careers as the business environment changes on a global scale. Managing in a sophisticated and complex global environment requires consistent high levels of performers and performance where I believe that no expense can be spared. Venturing into these emerging markets requires a tremendous amount of risk aversion, as well as a challenging and determined corporate disposition. You need to apply analytics, and thought leadership principles, when venturing into some markets that can be boom or bust depending on your strategy. Your corporate position needs to be examined to determine if these opportunities can be pursued. This venture needs to be viewed from a financial position, risk aversion, and leadership perspective. Emerging Markets are just that, third world countries that are emerging at a relatively high rate of speed, and the titans of industry are salivating in hot pursuit of these tremendous opportunities of growth and investment. These markets are Westernizing, and becoming hot beds of tremendous growth to the businesses that can penetrate and produce valuable products and services now becoming more in demand by these countries. Venturing into these markets is not an easy task; however, if your company is well positioned there can be a great financial windfall.

We will discuss in a later chapter the necessary means, as well as the problems and solutions to entering these markets. These opportunities in emerging markets are the Rubrics Cube of sophistication, requiring a very talented team of knowledge people, who can put all the colors in sequential order, and refine a strategy and plan of attack to capture these markets of opportunity. George Washington did not possess a highly sophisticated technology that could assist with decision-making and risk aversion statistical models. However, he did use his own intellect and determination, combined with a strategic vision and perseverance to unify and guide his troops. Entering emerging markets requires this vision and risk to gain your share of these markets.

In a football game, entering the red zone is the beginning of achieving the Holy Grail, which is the end zone. You are now entering that 20-yard line area and close to the prize. This is where the focus of the cameras and announcers are at their very best. The process and the grunt work of getting there, secure little attention, or are not as invigorating. This is a huge mistake made by many companies and businesses. Immediately, they want to enter these markets to gain and advantage, however, the grunt work and planning needed to secure these markets goes by the wayside. This can be catastrophic. That is why George Washington was so very successful in his leadership and vision. He planned and developed a strategy of attack, and promoted that plan to his troops. They trusted his leadership and abilities, and as I stated in an earlier chapter, saw the vision through his eyes. The titans of industry, who lead these billion dollar companies, need to practice these attributes when entertaining these markets. Yes, there is gold in these hills, still you need to meet the approach and strategy with perseverance and patience in order to secure the prize.

16 THE NEXT GENERATION ECONOMY
Challenges and Opportunities

There is an old adage commonly used called survival of the fittest. This phrase has been applied to sporting events, contests, talent competitions, and has now taken up residence in the business world especially where no barriers exist in a global competition. I am about to present to you a Rubrics Cube of sophisticated and interwoven challenges and opportunities in the current economy that I like to entitle a next generation economy.

This economy is not business as usual where corporations can rely on the stability of legacy products and complacency. Businesses must be consumers of a multitude of new ideas, technologies, and strategic involvement in risk laden emerging markets. The approach to this next generation economy must be a well thought out forward thinking aggressive involvement in market penetration, idea generation, and technological advancements. This next generation economy will be one of tremendous market complexities on a global level with a market mix of uncertainty and financial instability domestically and internationally. The current financial instability in the Euro Zones have presented the domino effect in countries with strong economies falling as less vibrant countries tumble and stumble against them. The International Monetary Fund has consistently been called to the round table in an attempt to bring fiscal solvency to the European Union to prevent cataclysmic fall out in the global market. countries that have practiced fiscal responsibility and shored up their economies have been called upon to assist in the financial restoration of these countries in self-preservation of their own stability. No one is safe or immune from these skeletons in the closet demonstrating that autonomy and imperialism as a sovereign country can no longer exist in the next generation economy.

Now that I have explained what I meant by the Rubrics cube of this economy one may ask, how do I solve this Rubrics cube in this next generation economy, and what does it mean to remain competitive in the business world today? I have explained in prior chapters the newest fog of business war that was initiated by this next generation economy. I cannot emphasize enough the visionaries and forward thinking leaders that will be required to navigate the fog. I believe that I am emphasizing this to the point of becoming the panacea of all corporate ills. To function in this next generation economy and maintain a sustained competitive advantage you must monitor the trending analysis of the business landscape continuously. Why all these action words; monitoring, thinking, evaluating, and performance? Simply because, as I stated earlier in the chapter, this next generation economy is a Rubrics cube of emerging markets, creative financing, and self imploding financial degradation in the Euro Zone which creates complexities that can be very challenging to unravel and reassemble. Business and corporate leaders must strategically piece together all these complexities strategically so that all the colors are coordinated in this next generation plan of attack. Let me now add another action word to the mix: Gutsy! You can massage that word anyway you need to customize your corporate culture, albeit, risk aversion, daring, or how about my favorite action word passion. This new economy requires a tremendous amount of passion and determination to navigate the ever-changing complexities and challenges. With that said, let's start to piece the Rubrics cube generation economy consumer, tastes and market conditions are going to change on an aggregate level. You cannot dissolve your legacy products and services, however, being a consumer and producer of new ideas will need to be the ground zero of your marketing plan. These new products and services will need to be introduced on a global platform, which will now include footprints on soil that you never navigated before. Gutsy, Right? Your mature corporation will now be experiencing growing pains maybe for the first time in many years. The new startups will be having the deer in the headlights look as they realize that the rainbow needs to have a bigger bow to reach the distant shores. Remaining in a small pond is no longer an option to reach a competitive and comparative advantage. Passion and determination must be the boat that you are riding on to explore these unchartered waters of opportunity. How will you market your products and services in a global landscape where one size does not fit all? Strategically you will need to monitor the market place domestically and internationally. What is trending? Is your legacy products and services still a viable commodity? How will you customize your products to fit the cultures and ever growing markets in that giant global market place that we call emerging markets? Now I did mention survival in the next generation economy and of course, I cannot be remiss in mentioning the fact that part of that economy still encompasses the domestic half of this great global marketplace. The elasticity and inelasticity of your products, supplies, and pricing may be affected or unaffected depending on whether you are in a domestic or international market environment, however, in this next generation economy there may be no dividing line in the sand and what happens on the global market platform now effects the entire marketplace like a tidal wave. If you have any reservations about this thought, just follow the daily markets with what is going on in Greece, Spain, and Italy. This next generation economy has also introduced market and distribution channel complexities into the mix of getting products to market quick, fast, and cost effectively.

Allow me to further explain. Product placement and distribution has changed with the tremendous advancements in technology. Distribution channels have now become technology channels. Third World Countries and emerging markets have unbelievably become technically perceptive in their use of the internet to purchase products and supplies on a global level. Exploring the topography of these markets goes far beyond the norms of scanning the physical environment for direct investment opportunities and barriers to entry. It has now shifted and positioned to an aggressive marketing structure with product development compliance according to the culture and needs, and formulated technical and physical channels of distribution. From a financial perspective, we also need to survey the landscape of the financial topography and diagnose any monetary considerations that need a considerable amount of analysis. Your assessment will need to determine if there has been a rise or fall in GDP and GNP growth within that country, as well as their fall out from the global recession. You will also need to determine whom their strategic alignments are with from a country-to-country analysis to determine stability and solvency. Remember, you are judged by the company you keep. The countries strength can be quickly dissolved by the businesses alliances, partnerships, and government infrastructure they espouse. The financial analysis will need a deep dive into the taxation and regulations of foreign investment as you attempt to gain a global footprint in the business arena. One only has to look at the complexities that have tidal waved Greece, and the rippling effects that it created in other markets. Remember, global investment is not a stand-alone initiative and the Black Hole of a fiscal cliff or destabilized governments can suck in a multitude of best efforts and pull your company apart. Companies that are exploring and navigating the global channels need to understand that this next generation economy is very congruent with Westernization and is now embodied in a wave of cultural appetites and material wants that meet or may at times exceed those of the United States.

Your marketing blitz must be tailored with meeting all these needs from a cultural perspective and assessing how to deliver these goods and services to a culture that is very similar to our domestic market, while very dissimilar in the way these goods and services are produced and manufactured. One must also survey the complexities that will be within the distribution channels and communication technology that will need to be streamlined and processed to meet your distribution activities and logistical units. Yes, there is much to gain in penetrating these markets and conversely much to lose if you do not leverage and analyze your strengths and assess your weaknesses to avoid the Black Hole of global positioning.

17 PREPARING FOR THE FOG OF BUSINESS WAR
Leadership, Communication, Performance, Branding

Now that we have covered from a performance and talent level what will be required to extend your business lifecycle and benchmark your competitive advantage against the competition, let us now examine the daily land mines and situations that can be catastrophic to your success. I call these the fog of business war. This is a very interesting concept that I will detail systematically. Over the last decade, we have heard much terminology regarding the fog of war coming from a perspective of the Middle East crisis. Our great military leaders, preparing their troops and their strategies for battle amidst a very unfamiliar terrain and culture also have to consider the plans and capabilities of the enemy, as well as their own abilities to gain a competitive advantage and succeed in their conquest.

This process is a composite of internal and external analysis of the overall situation as well as your opponent. In modern business, this would be the equivalent of an environmental scan. This can be a very daunting task that requires great vision and leadership, as well as a sixth sense at times. This very terminology called the fog of war, led me to do an extensive study on some of our great military leaders over the ages and to examine what were their great strengths and leadership abilities that enabled their great successes over their adversaries. How did they manage to get through this fog of war even during great trial and conflict? There is no magic potion, no invisible hand, and certainly no putting a finger in the wind and take an educated guess. These great individuals were visionaries, leaders, strategists and very determined to succeed. My thoughts continued to revisit these strategic lessons and the many successes of these great individuals and steered my studies in a direction of the current day economic and cultural challenges that are perplexing the many boardrooms and corporations today. Corporations are struggling to maintain a competitive advantage on a domestic and global level and set the high water mark of unbridled success. I feel that there is a great correlation between the strategies that were used in the fog of war by our great leaders, and the strategies that are required in the fog of the everyday business wars. Many challenges face businesses today such as globalizing your business to gain market share, economic down turns, taxation legislation, talent management in a multicultural market, and continuous technological advancements. When you combine these challenges with an ever-changing business landscape, this is where we can step into the fog of business war. Let us examine what I believe are ways and procedures to effectively navigate through this fog as we detail causes and effects of this fog and provide applications for continued success.

Let us first examine leadership. This term can never be loosely applied to placing a person in a position and saying; take over, your in charge. The diverse business arena is made up of a very complex system of vision, thought leadership, market changes, change management, and an entrepreneurial spirit. A leader must be knowledgeable on technology, trending markets, and globalized opportunities. The complexities of modern business involve a certain amount of risk aversion complimented with a daringness to tread where others will not follow. Success in the global business economy is having the vision and leadership to explore opportunities concentrated in Developing Countries, Emerging Markets, Europe, Asia, Far East, Middle East, and Central and South America. Some leaders just shoot from the hip and jump right in with a direct investment in the global opportunity that they are exploring. 'Build baby build' is the mantra; we are the first ones on the block. This adventurism is very admirable, however, what are the thought leadership processes that went into the decision? Due to global expansion in the marketplace, corporations are being thrust into a new fog of business war just to remain competitive.

These new opportunities also bring major challenges to your business model and branding. The fog of business war can start immediately when a company has a business model of maintaining their position and product suites in a domestic market. This may have been your easy street, well sold legacy products in a domestic legacy market. Then reality sets in during the viewing of the Quarterly Reports, and the ROI and financials have seemed to dramatically slip. Let us look back to my earlier statement concerning the importance of visionary leaders and an environmental scanning. No one can fall asleep at the proverbial wheel while the next generation economic changes in product tastes, and business cultural changes pass you by. Now the heavy fog arrives, what do you do next? What new markets must you entertain? Do you retool or abandon the legacy product lines? Can I afford the Research and Development to increase my product sets? How do I culture my products to fit the current International markets? Lastly, into what markets do I and can I afford to expand? Well, I will try to avoid redundancy, however, as my earlier chapters expressed, you need to secure talent with leadership and vision. The quality and vision of this talent should assist your business in keeping your finger on the pulse of the next generation economy as well as the economics that tags along as the rider.

Let me express some interesting philosophies that will assist in hitting a pot hole while in the fog of the business wars. You will always need a cash cow of legacy products that you can fall back on to have cash flow liquidity in order to hopefully maintain a positive cash flow on the ledger books. This positive cash flow can assist you in establishing after expense cash reserves for product development and research into global expansion possibilities. Now, this is not a short-term strategy but remember the old adage that haste makes waste. Do not abandon your domestic market or legacy products, but consider retooling them possibly in the design and packaging as well as the ever-important quality element as societal needs grow and change exponentially. Please remember, society and tastes are changing dramatically and a new look to and old friend as well as updated advertising is necessary. Even if the product is twenty years old, a fresh look, and a make over so to speak, and some savvy marketing will enable you to maintain considerable market share of your domestic cash cow. Financial frugality and intelligent spending in the right areas will assist your business in the research and development areas of product development and global research.

Let us apply the look before you leap technique. Understand that global expansion can be a heavy fog to navigate through in the daily competitive business wars. You first need to perform an internal SWOT analysis to have a clearly defined idea on your risk aversion and financial position. You will also need to assess your overall talent pool, which I might say should have always been positioned as top level no matter the level of the position. Conceptually, even with top talent, entering into global markets will task you with acquiring a talent leadership with a global vision and a keen sense of the International markets. You will also need to perform a SWOT analysis on your competition that may be entering these global markets, their strengths, financial position, what markets they are entering, and with what product they will be entering these markets. Outside of financial positioning, you will now be examining your global positioning possibilities. Remember as a child, your mother always said, 'if your friend jumps off the bridge, does that mean you will jump'? Exercise extreme caution and only penetrate these markets when you have the whole plan in place. No knee jerk reactions or hunches, or the throw of the dice will work here. By no shape or form do you need to simultaneously create and go off your own fiscal cliff. With these examinations, the fog will begin to clear.

Now, what markets do you enter? Well, your research should determine what markets will roll out the welcome mat, and if and when they do, you will need to examine the cultural variations that you will need to fit that market. These examinations will include ingredients, if the product is a consumable commodity, and how it will fit and service the cultural climate of your global market. When you stretch your own legacy products outside of the current domestic arena, even they will have to possibly be retooled to fit the culture of your new market in the global arena. Financially, global expansion can be a costly horizon. That is why your own financial position needs to be evaluated and estimated. This will be your knock before you enter, and even with limited financial resources or deep pockets of reserves, these financial resources can be immediately dried up if not allocated properly as you finance this expedition. A pricing mechanism will need to be placed in good order in accordance with the market that you are entering. This can be readily researched and developed by reviewing the estimated annual incomes of the country, and the purchasing power of the population. Now, there are many factors that play into the equation such as government taxation, and cost of living. These figures can be substantially higher or lower in accordance with developed or Third World countries. Other factors that will need to be considered is whether to have a physical direct investment in that country, or simply to maintain a supply and demand relationship with your suppliers, manufactures, and vendors in that country. Either plan invites its own set of issues and responsibilities especially if you are a unionized company, need we go any further with that. To summarize this point, you will need to estimate the costs of entering that country, the product pricing to accommodate the average incomes of that country, and if you will be on the negative or positive side of the cash flow. These are just a sampling of the fog of business wars and solutions that you will need to consider and prepare for when entering these markets, however, please keep these business tips in mind when dealing in our current domestic markets, as they are getting more complex as societies needs grow and change. In the next chapter, I will discuss additional solutions to other global penetration complexities.

18 GOING GLOBAL
Intended or Emergent Strategy?

In the strategic marketplace of business where the Gladiators and Titans of industry do battle for corporate leadership and power rankings, the white board generally will have the terms Multinational or Global as part of their corporate success mapping in their quest for the Golden Fleece. Is this the intended or emergent strategy of your company, or was this executive decision made by holding a finger in the air to measure the velocity of the winds of change? Is risk aversion considered, or was this decision made by jumping on the market express. Expansion or over expansion cannot be a knee jerk reaction, nor can it be a company who decides to flex their corporate muscle in the global arena. Successful companies know that decisions on this level require critical mass decision making and a total internal and external analysis of their competencies. An environmental scan of the global arena can provide the determinants and the logistical analysis needed to craft a decision that will successfully aid in this decision making process. Companies sometimes make their global footprint decision on hedging against a lack luster domestic market.

Reflecting back to earlier chapters, I consistently insist on leadership with vision as a primary focus of successful and consistently great companies. Visionary leadership with a sixth sense of business acumen and a high level of knowledge and expertise is and always will be essential to competitive sustainability. Critical thinking and high emotional intelligence will lead a company to heights less travelled. Making decisions on a Multinational or Globalized footprint will take a composite level of thinking, as many factors will need to be considered in the process.

Let us examine a few of the layers of decisions that need to be made. We discussed in previous chapters that many companies are attempting to gain a geographic footprint and a sustained competitive edge by entering into the emerging market segment. First in line in these countries and their increasingly growing markets have become high traffic areas for profits and a diversified target market mix. These are high-risk horizons due to the lack of infrastructure, cultural variations, and many unknowns in the governmental structure. There needs to be a great risk aversion to consider entering into these infantile markets of opportunity. With this in mind, many companies take the road to the more mature and stabilized markets of Europe and the Middle and Far East. Earlier in this chapter, I stated that many companies enter into these markets to hedge against a lackluster domestic market that can be suffering from taxation, labor unions, and high and consistent levels of unemployment that erodes discretionary income and inflates future uncertainty. In previous chapters, I discussed how companies small and large are redefining strategies with the focus being on expansion and penetration into globalization and emerging markets. How do we do it? How do we plan strategies? How do we finance this expedition of sailing into these new horizons? The less financially endowed have to look inwardly and be introspective as to their immunity to risk aversion while others have started to look into merger or acquisition opportunities to enhance their business model, expand their global footprint, and shore up their financial position. What is the prescription to adequately enter these world markets? What pitfalls does your business have to examine in order to avoid a total collapse, and if the green light is on, how do I successfully carry out this venture?

Well, let us start out with mergers and acquisitions. Many companies, who want to run with the big dogs and penetrate these global markets, decide to merge or acquire another company to increase product sets or, gain a larger footprint in the global arena. Generally, this is an emergent strategy, one either for increased profitability, or to gain a competitive edge against their competition. There are many ways to look into accomplishing this feat, and many different areas that will need examined to have a successful merger or acquisition and avoid a collapse. Lets us start with a plan to merge with another company and demonstrate how this can be successfully accomplished in a systematic process. The best way is to start from the beginning with this strategy. Mergers are a two way street as you have to be as appealing to the other party as they need to be to you. Let us start with the emergent strategy of merging with another from a financial perspective. First, you need to do the credit check as part of your due diligence. This will be the first stage of your external SWOT analysis on the company that you intend to merge with. Remember, that you want to gain a competitive edge in the global arena, not a financial implosion. This area of analysis should not be taken lightly, and an intelligent suggestion should be to hire forensic accountants to scour the books for financial liquidity and stability. Your company should not only look at the financial stability of the partner in the merger, but one also needs to look at the cash reserves, payables, receivables, total assets versus liabilities as part of your check list. Checking the corporate investments that the partner may have, as well as if they are global holdings or basically domestic, and in what companies or investment firms these investments are being held is essential. Bad investments can erode financial assets very quickly. Another sanitizing of the financial data needs to be in the area of labor contracts if they apply or the compensation packages of C level executives in order to review the total allocation of financial resources. I am not opposed in anyway to appropriate compensation packages for your knowledge people, or the leadership at the helm, however, one needs to be sure that the productivity of these personal qualifies for the package. In relationship to this is a need to examine the organizational grid for redundant and over lapping operations in order to prevent a top-heavy financial drain on expenditures. I spoke in a previous chapter on the fog of business war from a competitive standpoint in the business arena. Entering into a merger or acquisition can be a very tedious operation that also carries the fog of business war into the mix. This fog is a very internal fog that can take place during the transition period. The reason that I call this an internal fog is that your company or business is going into this merger or acquisition to position your business to lead the pack and beat the competition in the global marketplace. So allow me to clear that fog so to speak, and discuss the potholes of these transitions and provide valuable solutions to asphalt over these bumps on your road to success.

Let us begin from an operations perspective as we hope to bring a synergy from two organizations that will hope to successfully and symbiotically blend their strategies and talent pools to achieve and acquire a global dominance. This will need to be clearly viewed from thirty thousand feet from the C level to the floor level to make this a smooth and seamless transition. Two different corporate cultures must be aligned to accomplish a single vision and strategy, and how is this accomplished? First, total communication and a defined and shared strategic plan and vision are the genesis of this endeavor. Whether you are a small business or a giant gladiator, this process cannot be skipped. There is a very uncomfortable feeling at the beginning of this relationship like two strangers meeting for the first time. Why do I insist on communication? Let's examine the importance of relationship building, and to share the empirical knowledge between these two new partners to align the strategic initiative. The organizational grid and the leadership will need to be clearly defined and communicated to all personal in a very transparent manner with no veils or confusion. This will need to be a very streamlined and seamless operation to avoid down time and loss of morale to the personal as ambiguity and change can stall the overall operational procedures as change is difficult and uncertainty additionally creates confusion. Therefore, to reiterate from the C level to the floor level communication is vital in this process. Once the strategy is defined and refined decisions will need to be made as to the vertical leaders and managers who will be the decision heads at all the vital areas of operations from domestic operations to off shore global operations. The technology vertical will also need to be shored up appropriately with the knowledge and management personnel in place, as this will be the aggregate level of communication in real time on a global platform. The next step in this process is from a human resources perspective. In a global market, mergers and acquisitions that you tie in with can be either domestic, global, or both, as off shoring is a staple that is vital to remain competitive in the global business arena. The challenge will be how to mix and blend these cultural and ethnic differences together to successfully carry out the strategic initiatives that were drawn up on the white board in the C Suite. There is a solution to remedy this rubrics cube, and mix all these cultures together in a very quick time to assist in this hopefully seamless transition while preventing costly confusion and downtime. Successfully completing this transition with minimum potholes will require a tremendous blending of knowledge personnel from both entities who could quickly carry the ball. These knowledge personnel must be very in tune with cultural sensitivities as well as facilitating your strategic plans in your global basin. This will definitely require a financial investment in travel and training in these countries, which will become a necessity as your personnel blend the strategy and culture into a beautiful mosaic of knowledge sharing and cultural awareness. Through a very thorough training and development program, this knowledge could be transferred through webinar training programs, and cultural sensitivity learning tools that will reduce the stress of a changed social and corporate culture. This training will also need to include training in communication and language, as well as body language and non-verbal communications that can pose problems when merging into international countries. In addition, when the merger and acquisition entails a direct investment in another country, many decisions will need to be made regarding if domestic employees will be working off shore as well as international's working in domestic operations. These transitions need careful observations and micro management to a point. Therefore, in summation, there will technically be two transitions that will need to be fine-tuned in the merger and acquisition incubation. The first is the blending of two corporate cultures that can have varying degrees of cultures and styles such as bureaucratic, regimented, laid back or fast paced. This can be a tricky transition, as the defined culture will need to be modified in order to have a very symbiotic and successful relationship. Secondly the global culture will need to utilize the processes and techniques that I fore-mentioned. These techniques will smooth the fall out from the strategic alliance of this merger and acquisition, and shore up the key to your success, which is your human resources team. To integrate another key point in the merger and acquisition process, continuous strategic commitment and early planning must be carried out in order to catch and ride the wave quickly and integrate promptly. The next generation economy and global positioning is happening quickly and in almost real time. What seems like a great strategic move one minute can be obsolete the next.

In my earlier chapters, I discussed the meaning and culture of a next generation economy where consumer tastes and desires are evolving quickly, as well as, the attributes of the economy are moving and changing exponentially with it. Taxation, corporate financing of new ventures, and fallout from the recession as well as the tightening of government regulations on corporate and individual borrowing has created a noose around society and corporations. However, this is part of the next generation economy, and with it, corporate governance and due diligence has been micro managed. Consumer demands have now shifted consumer needs where discretionary funds are now focused on sustenance instead of luxury. This will be the narrow margins that your merger and acquisition will need to reflect on, so a need to leverage your best corporate attributes will need to be scanned. Internal scanning of both parties will need to be compared and contrasted in order to determine if this will be a profitable strategy in order to gain a global prominence and sustainable advantage.

Lastly, as part of your merger and acquisition, you will need to have an in-depth look at your global platform of technology. You will be having many feeds and communication transfers coming from around the globe as you blend your software and communication systems into a fusion of cultures. Symbiosis will be the key, as not only will language barriers need to be correlated, but also a mutual understanding of knowledge transfer and fluid information. This will take early planning and a cohesive management team on both sides of the globe to blend cultures and erase deficiencies. These are principles that will need to be treated internally and strategically. However, your product, pricing, and external cultural sensitivities, as well as aligning your marketing and advertising to fit and compliment rigorous religious and societal customs will need to be dramatically addressed.

19 MODELING YOUR BUSINESS
An Internal and External Affair

Executives in the boardroom plan strategies, marketing promotions, and niche products that will hopefully place their company as the benchmark of their business arena. They plan and develop their customized product sets focusing on target markets, international penetration, and instant return on investment. In many cases, this is the focus for how they build and construct their business model. I would be remiss in stating the fact that this is not only an important component of building a business model, but is also essential for the survival of any business. With this preface stated, I would like to highlight upon another essential component of building a successful business model. Although branding a business model is generally considered an external affair of product development, market niches, and successful market penetration, there is another component that needs to be considered in the branding process, which is your human capital. This is the most important part of any successful model, and is sometimes estranged from the process of modeling the business for success. Much time and efforts are spent on the external affairs, and the internal modeling is disconnected from the process. I feel that this concept needs further explanation to clarify the reasoning behind my philosophy. I have heard employees who work for a successful business say, they made their money off the sweat of our backs without any concern for our needs or us. You may glean from this statement that the business was still successful, however, a consistent eroding of and discontent for your human capital will eventually rear its terrible head. There is a consistent need to brand and model your business internally and externally for longevity and for extending your play in the business arena. Employees are the conduit that links a successful business to consistent success and market growth and stability.

Allow me to provide another example of my business model philosophy. Over the years of watching major league baseball, I have seen major league team owners consistently build successful teams on the concept of great player retention and a determination to be champions for the long run. They have built financial stability and marketability from placing a great product on the field and simultaneously being open and fair to their players. This is a basic equation, and branding and modeling requires a check and balance of internal and external components to build that successful business entity. Leaving any of these elements out will be like a house of cards, and will tumble fast. Behavioral science states that the hierarchy of needs is prevalent in human nature. We go from basic needs to growth and development needs. Through the stages of our lives, these needs change and grow as the culture of society changes and grows. Just as a business changes and grows according to market needs and economic changes, employee development expands to meet their own societal and economic variations. Your business model needs to prepare for reset economies, uncertain markets, styles and trends, as well as customizable product development as insatiable consumer appetites change and expand. Boardroom strategies, marketing plots, and trend analysis through statistical information is sifted through in order for a business to be the best on the block and be the model for all others. The time and attention spent on these efforts must also be extended to the consideration of employee development, performance management, training and development, and basic attention to the human element. This is successful modeling of your business internally and externally, and when they cohesively collaborate what a model it will be. You will make it through downturns, reset economies, and the rough patches of the business cycle.

Let us now refine the process of branding and modeling your business or corporation from a perspective of internal focus of target business to customer satisfaction. When I talk in this book about having a due diligence of ethics and responsibility to the customer and your employees, this is a point to be taken very seriously. Having a mission statement and a business model goes well beyond having an introverted ideology of self-preservation. This also entails focusing your model on customer responsibility and satisfaction. Now let me expand on this philosophy a little deeper as to clarify my intent. A mission statement and a business model needs to focus on presenting your goods and services in the most economical pricing structures complimented with quality goods and services. Wow, one may say, what about my ROI and my profit structure? This seems like a one-way street. Well, let's take a concise look at the alternative. I have seen companies with a mission statement that could have qualified for a Pulitzer Prize promising social responsibility along with quality goods and services at a very economical price. When the audit is done on sales, service, and profits, a very discouraging report is presented. Obviously, there was a disconnect between the mission statement, the business model, and the service that was presented. Many promises may draw in customers, however, the products and services will create a revolving door. There was mismatch between your business strategy and promises made. With that said, your business model must be clearly focused on creating value for the customer as well as your business. This is the vital link in the long chain of your business success and extending the play of your sustainability and longevity.

There are many ways that a company or even a small business can establish a business model. It can be modeled on technology, distribution channels, suppliers and vendor relationships as well as global footprint. This modeling process is a great genesis in positioning your company against the competition as being the best in the business. Modeling does not happen overnight, and cannot be a knee jerk reaction to consumer trends. This has to be a carefully thought out process utilizing your overall corporate strengths. For a technology business model to be successful, you will need to build your software and technology suite to augment your goods or services that you provide. You will have to secure a technology driven base of intellectuals and knowledge employees to drive this technology model that is the driver of your business strategy. Now this technology does not necessarily have to be the product or service that you are selling, however, it needs to always point in the direction of your customer base as a means of creating value and cost effectiveness. Conversely, if this technology is your product or service to your customers, then your model could be one of securing the highest quality components and architecture from your suppliers that will deliver the best in class technology equipment. If your technology is a service or software, your model could be built around the quality of your knowledge people and engineers who develop this product or service. Once again, this model needs to be focused on the customer or customers that you service.

I use terminology throughout this book describing the fog of business wars. I present much thought to this concept as I steered its meaning to assist businesses in this next generation economy. The fog of business wars has many elements and challenges in a just in time consumer trending market paired with changing demands and tastes. This fog is not localized; it has a global covering from a perspective of companies now operating on a worldwide platform. Trends, consumer demands, and tastes are now on an aggregate level as businesses seek to position and extend their presence on a global level. How does this fog affect the process of modeling your business in this next generation economy? The simple response is because the market trends and competition becomes so complex that setting a strategy in place to navigate through the fog without a clear navigation plan can set paralysis in place as you decide what model will best suit the economy and marketplace. Going forward in successfully modeling your business, you will need to identify and leverage your corporate strengths in conjunction with creating value and quality for your customers.

20 ETHICS FOR YOUR BUSINESS LIFECYCLE
Best Business Practice

I would be remiss not to add this important chapter. Best business practices are vital for the longevity of any business from a mom and pop store to a global corporation. One would have to been under a rock to miss the rise and fall of some of the most dominant giants in the global arena. They were the top players, and the cream of the crop. Now these iconic corporations of America have closed their doors, and Do Not Enter signs appear where Mission Statements use to be displayed. Dried up mulch now replaces beautiful flowerbeds that graced the entrances of these businesses.

Best business practices are often viewed as a research process, in which a business or corporation discovers and refines the best way to manufacture a product, and provide a service. One misguided ethical decision and the results can be fatal. Some businesses decide to push the envelope to the extent that they will never be caught, or that crafty worded explanations utilizing extreme sophist tactics will guise the real intent. I have intentionally massaged this phrase of best business practices to ethics for your business lifecycle to provocatively stimulate your thought processes in the reasoning that this is the summation of all performance. If you knew that I was leading you in that direction, you probably would agree that utilizing these best practice ethic methods is the only way to go. In the quest for the golden road of profiteering, the ethical vision can become much clouded and obscured leading to a loss of integrity and rash decision-making processes. Sarbanes Oxley if not the redemptive force of ethics maintenance has led to a rethinking process when considering stepping out of bounds. Sarbanes Oxley law has provided the do and don't checklist, as well as the ramifications and results of unethical actions. Please do not limit the imagination only to the fall of major corporations and their accounting and bookkeeping problems, best practices also involve ADA compliance, Title VII law, EEO activity, as well as wage and hour practices. A lack of compliance and awareness in these areas can and may lead to legal action and major lawsuits that can be the demise of your business or company.

Let me not forget to mention the major D word that we all attempt to avoid, and that is discrimination. A business has to be very judicious concerning this very delicate area. Due diligence has to be the best practice methodology concerning all these issues, and as far as performance is concerned a consistent monitoring and evaluating must be conducted to ensure consistent compliance. I have witnessed major corporations being caught at disability discrimination costing close to 100 million dollars in settlement and litigation costs. We must envision the · monetary consequences of these actions, and the public image that has been tarnished in full view of the general public who are our customers. These unethical practices also result in a loss of credibility with other business partners. The leaders and managers of corporations and business must be responsible in all business activity to present an example of best practices and guidance to all employees. Practicing ethical responsibility should be the highlight of every mission statement, and the guiding light of your business. This is not rocket science. Moreover, this is just a plain common sense approach that can provide a continuum for the long-range success of your business, and always should be the major part of your strategic planning and performance enhancement planning. Every functional department and component of your company needs to be instilled with these principles and practices to maintain a level of high productivity and consistency. Performance may fail, strategy may at times decline, but these can be revised and retooled, however, best business practices when maintained will never fail your business in the long run. Let us examine this subject further to enhance the vital importance of ethics and business integrity. Some businesses and corporations will hang their ethical standards on the wall for all employees to be overwhelmed with the company's vital concern, and consistent vigilance with this issue of ethical compliance. The failure enters when the actions of leadership and management are far from being consistent with the philosophical standards in the employee handbook and mission statement. This action is a double edge sword that will take your company down on many levels. First, illegal actions or non-compliance of legal standards will topple the company externally and internally. The collateral damage will be the employee base-jumping off ship for brighter horizons. Ethical responsibility goes well beyond internal functionality of your business practices; it also extends to the well being of your employees as well as social responsibility.

21 LEAD BY EXAMPLE
Do As You Say

The first fatal error that will turn your business inside out is to not lead by example. Through the conversations around the water cooler rumors begin to circulate, and when there is negative activities going on within the company especially at the management or C suite level rumors spread like fire. Once getting started, this fire is hard to extinguish. One only needs to look at the corporate governance at major corporations who are in hot water to have empirical evidence of a company falling from grace with ethical problems. Maximizing and optimizing your human capital begins with leading by example, and as stated in my rules for proper construction of a mission statement, say what you mean and do what you say. This attitude, through good business osmosis will inebriate through the entire company and will enhance the competitive energy of your human capital. With the right fit of human capital, meaning those with leadership abilities and a willingness to learn and promote the strategic vision of the company, employees can be empowered and energized to perform at a higher level then expected when the leadership has an ethical policy and a participative style of management.

Let's for a moment reflect back to the leadership style of George Washington. When engaging in battle, he did not selectively choose the conflicts that he would be involved in. When the going got tough, he got tougher. He had no C Suite to watch the battle action, and had no webinar to provide a consistent flow of real time information for decision-making or strategic development. The business arena can be a battlefield, and without proper leadership a mutiny can take place as well as desertion of your greatest asset, your human capital. Tough economic times can develop a theory of leadership complacency. There is a danger of espousing to a sense of archaic behavior and management by fear concepts that develop from a tight job market. Where can they go? They have to be here, so do as I say and not as I do. Trust me, this system does not work and usually even in a tight economy desertion will take place. Earlier we discussed the fog of war, and how proper leadership and strategic vision clears the air and the fog. Economic downturn, tight credit markets, and consumer uncertainty is in a business sense the fog of business war that can permeate throughout your business. Strong leadership with a focus on ethics and principles will make this fog easier to navigate through. This preparation does not turn on a dime, but is embedded in the DNA of the cultural and philosophical attitudes of the management. Great corporations can develop an attitude of infallibility, but one only needs to look at the Titanic and the great Roman Empire. Some thought that it could not sink, and some thought that it could not be defeated. One deficiency brought them down, poor leadership. Size does not matter; it is the smallest and weakest link in the chain that can be your demise. This attitude and philosophy does not happen overnight or at a level of situational management needed on the spur of a moment. It is your mission statement, your management, your human capital, your business DNA, but most of all your standard of ethics and principles. Great leaders have never left the trenches even in their darkest moments. Constant promotion of ethical standards, and leading by good example from the C suite on down have turned around the most drastic situations that have sent companies on a downward spiral.

22 THE KEYS TO YOUR BUSINESS LONGEVITY
Transparency, Communication, Modeling, Performance

Often times in the corporate arena, Transparency, Communication, Modeling, and Performance, the vital elements of success and longevity, are highly overlooked and undervalued. Transparency is often viewed as a specter in the attic, and a policy of silence is golden takes on a completely new meaning. Corporate communiqués are consistent and constant; however, is the entire story told to the employee base, or only what you want them to hear? Performance is preached on the bully pulpit, but consequently when training budgets are set the resources in this area are very streamlined and downsized.

To extend the play and lifecycle of your company an internal audit of these four components need to be accounted for. Starting in the area of communication, this is an area of vital importance, and water cooler talk should not be the source of encoding and decoding valuable information to the employee base. A common problem is that many companies and businesses often times are concerned about the sensitivity and value of the information that needs to be disseminated to the employee. This results in the shadowing and retaining of valuable information that may be of vital importance to your human capital. Competitive sustainability is the monarch and key to your business's success and longevity, and without consistent and accurate communication being shared and addressed throughout the corporate grid from top to bottom it will certainly lead to disaster. Communication is even more prevalent during times of economic crisis and uncertainty in the global business arena. Many corporations and businesses have been impacted and disrupted by rogue waves in the sea of business tranquility, which has brought their strategic planning to a screeching halt while disrupting short and long-term goals. With this disruption, sustaining competitive advantage in the business arena needs to be immediately revitalized, and fluid lines of communication need to be maintained and managed. Generally, businesses need to always have a plan B and C as a backup to act as a conduit for continued strategic mobility. The important element that needs to be consistent with all planning is transparent and consistent communication to all levels of the corporate grid. I cannot emphasize enough this important aspect to all corporate leaders and managers as the catalyst to right the ship when the rogue wave hits. The culture that usually germinates in this hectic environment is one of chaos and fragmented communication. Meetings will be called, but many times only to voice the damage that has been done to the corporate environment, as well as the downsizing that needs to be implemented, and changes that will need to take place. Change, now there is the more ominous word. It strikes fear and uncertainty throughout the entire company as employees begin the processing of what change means to them and the company. The dollar value placed on lost productivity in this type of environment is staggering to the imagination, and regaining that financial strength is difficult to make up. I cannot emphasize the importance of strategic preparation and backup planning that should be the blueprint in all business environments from small concerns to corporate giants. This strategy and corporate planning, needs to be communicated at all times to all employees to reduce the down time when economic uncertainty hits. I like to compare this to a typical fire drill procedure. When employees are called to a fire drill safety program, they are provided with the entire safety plan such as exits and directions on what procedures to follow. They are not provided with only half the plan or chaos would break out, and injuries or even death may occur. This should be the same process to follow with corporate communication by always delivering all the information, and inform them of the when, where, why and how. This will not only provide the corporate blueprint, but will also road map the direction the company is going. This will act as a preventive process to uncertainty, as well as stabilize the environment with a sustained competitive advantage. Transparency and communication are the vital keys to business vitality, and a healthy corporate environment for increased performance of your human capital. Does this take maximum effort, you bet, but so does raising a sinking ship once it hits the ocean floor. Corporations pride themselves on building major transformational teams, leading change teams, and quality circles that are to right the ship in the midst of economic peril and uncertainty as they ride the wave of the global business arena. Thought leaders and forward thinkers construct major white papers on corporate and cultural effectiveness that will enhance the productivity of human capital.

With all this in mind, let us add to the mix the staggering amount of technological advancement going on in the communication software arena. Communication can travel around the globe in a nanosecond bringing the world to the door of your business. CEO's can board the corporate jet traveling to the Middle East while virtually attending a meeting thousands of miles from their destination. With this image in mind, why do so many companies fall due to lack of information and communication presented to their employee base? Why is critical information left out of the company meetings when it would best serve the human capital base to have knowledge of this vital information? It all goes back to my preface that it can be taboo to provide constant and continuous information to the greatest source of productivity, your human capital. This is the thought processes of many managers and leaders that too much information can ruin the company. I do agree that some information needs to be kept discreet; however, I am discussing the vital channel of information that needs to be transmitted that often falls silent. I firmly believe that communication dissemination falls within a sphere of influence, and I would like to elaborate further on this thought process.

There is a reality in the business culture that I believe is either ontological or a learned process that prohibits management from cycling information to all vital channels. We have more means of communication transfer available to us today then in any other time in history; however, it is very dependent upon the quality of information and the proper channels that it reaches. Businesses runs on an aggregate level, and on a global platform. The influx of information and the quality and reliability of that information has to be filtered, organized, and transferred to the proper channels in a logical manner. The business arena is a very sophisticated and complex grouping of international and domestic operations with a tremendous reliance on adequate information from various cultures and business units around the globe. Streamlining and making sense of this informational stream is vital in decision-making processes for strategic planning and split second decisions that need to be made to maintain business fluidity. No one can fall asleep at the wheel, as one slip can be catastrophic. Logical organization and the conciseness of the information needs to be a priority of utmost concern. What if the information is very ambiguous and unclear? For example, before deciding to make a direct investment in an emerging market country, your international consultants are attempting to gather as much information as possible on the countries culture, barriers to entry, and niche markets. This may be a very daunting task if information is vague, inaccurate and christened with uncertainty. How do we make accurate judgments and assessments based on ambiguous and unclear information? How do we plan strategies and market penetrations to gain competitive advantage? There are no simple answers, however, there are solutions. Maintaining accurate informational streams requires informational cleansing where prevailing attitudes and assumptions as well as thought bias cannot be permitted, which will only allow distortions and irrelevance in the thought leadership processes. There must be a decision tree of informational processing that will cleanse and sanitize irrelevancy, pruning away misconceptions and knee jerk decision-making, allowing the most logical conclusion to prevail. Through this information cleansing process, and pairing it with proper research on your strategic plan, ambiguities will be eliminated. Harkening back to the strategy of market penetration into an emerging market country, the reliability of information in a very ambiguous environment, with cross cultural differences and language barriers can prove very difficult. Increased market research into these developing countries accented with defined structural lines of communication flow will result in fluidity and reliability of communication, as you will turn the corner with better peripheral vision. Transparency and defined communication processes are only part of the strategy in extending the play and lifecycle of your business; however, these are not the legs that you can stand on alone. You will need to define your business model and the plateaus that you intend to stand on as the pinnacle of excellence. Modeling your business is a very detailed process and needs examined from an aggregate level internally and externally. Without stepping to introversion, it is imperative that a SWOT analysis needs to be achieved at an internal level in conjunction with your strategic planning processes. Normally, the first initiative that every business wants to embark on from a new startup to a mature legacy business is to scan the external environment by way of the infamous SWOT analysis. Utilizing this process to identify target markets, defining trends, and examining threats in their business arena becomes paramount to introspectively analyzing their greatest asset, human capital. Stating in earlier chapters, your human capital is the plasma that runs the corporate engine and no strategy is ready for launching without defining leadership and talent management processes. This is the part of branding and modeling of your business that at times is left undefined. You have polished the coat of arms while the inside decays.

In my research on reorganization, restructuring, and retooling of companies as they attempt to stretch their horizons into multinational boundaries while competing in a very elastic economy the challenges become even more complex. I like to title this economy a next generation economy for various reasons. The current structure of leveraging your business on financing, market expansion, tax structures, and global penetration is now being redefined as new legislative processes, and aggregate global consumer demands change. Direct investments internationally become more complex as currencies fluctuate during tumultuous uprisings in certain countries. These are now the demands placed on businesses in this next generation economy that we are now experiencing as the reset economy shakes out. This collectively will result in old business models being recycled into more lean, more aggressive business models as they compete for that high water benchmark. The need for business leaders to micro manage these changes and redefine strategies with a great mix of talent management is the recipe for success. Decision making on both sides of the globe will need to be accomplished. The critical thinking processes needed to gain leverage in global markets must be in real time with a vision to the future to ascertain a high performance standard. To elaborate on this process further, real time decisions is a requirement as market economies, consumer trends, and currency fluctuations change on a dime. That is why I continue to name this current global market with all its' moving parts, a next generation economy. The markets have never moved and changed as fast as they are now in this new century. In past economies, businesses had adequate time to respond to consumer tastes and demands. Legacy products had a longer shelf life, and your product set could subsist with one or two mainstays and still set the high water mark for competition. No longer, what was popular today is gone tomorrow, and research and development are constantly attempting to reinvent the wheel or give it a different purpose. What creates success in this next generation economy is performance and more performance, and of course teaming up with high-level performers. This economic culture that businesses now deal with is all part of the fog of business war. This economic culture creates a haze over many businesses as they struggle to battle all the consistent complexities that they need to navigate through. In light of all this haze, the four keynote processes of transparency, communication, modeling, and performance is the winds needed to disperse the fog. Communicating the strategy to all hands on deck is vital as your company expands their global footprint, and the strategy is made clear to all your components. Strategically, this becomes even more necessary as you cross cultural barriers and your human capital becomes more diversified. Crossing cultural barriers with patriots and human capital from various countries where you entertain business opportunities can be a very daunting task as shared knowledge and strategy needs to be refined and sifted to have a singular meaning and vision to all employees. Transparency needs to also be taken quite seriously, as communicating the message must pervade overall to run successfully with no missing links in the chain. Your modeling process needs to be flexible to meet the challenges and markets that you are attempting to penetrate, meaning that the model that you are leveraging must be strategically adaptable to your product set and your customers as a shared value.

23 THE GOAL LINE

There is not a magic potion to ensure business success. Six Sigma with its standard deviation principles, can monitor quality standards but not promise longevity. Global footprints, metrics analysis, emerging market industrialization, great compensation packages, and employee incentives are all important; however, these are no replacement for ethics in business or leadership by principles. This is organic and growing, a philosophy that gives life to a business and takes on a life of its own. It promotes a culture of self worth and empowerment. Success in this philosophy is part of the human condition that Maslow discussed in his hierarchy of needs principles.

As the economy has weakened and competition has become fierce in the battle for more customers with less discretionary dollars, this has created the perfect storm in the competitive business arena. These storms can at times create situational management in the areas of ethical standards and best business practices. With mounting job losses on a daily basis, ethical business practices can go out the window in an attempt to cover tracks of mistakes or get inventive with the bottom line numbers in order to secure their positions. The current downturn in our economic climate has led to very creative ways in violating ethical standards and best practice methodologies in an attempt to stay employed at the expense of others. Owners conceiving unethical practices to keep the company afloat in the positive light of investors, while in reality the business is sinking fast. Skimming money from the profits, while reflecting the amount in the infamous miscellaneous expenses column of the ledger to balance the books. These are principles that will never need to be trained or developed. Best business practices must be a mandatory part of every strategic initiative, and objective of your business; any other strategy is a plan to fail. The goal line of every company should be applying best business practices, and business ethics in conjunction with selecting the highest level of performers who are consistent forward thinking leaders and visionaries with a desire for success. This plan will embrace every strategy and business plan that actuates out of the boardroom, and should be the whiteboard philosophy embedded in all your employees from the receptionist to the C

Level. Please remember, every employee is a link in your chain of success, and even the strongest link can be broke by the weak. You must always create an environment of inclusiveness where everyone and their ideas are welcomed, and considered in the grand strategy of the company. The Mission Statement must be your mantra and not just a decorated poster on the wall. Do not be frugal with your knowledge people. Always recognize and award your employees for the success of the company. Take time to listen to employee concerns and empower their ideas, and when possible have an open door of communication; this will prevent the revolving door. Always treat all employees with the utmost respect, and create no caste system within the corporate castle. These chapters contain the policies and procedures that you will need to put into practice in order to gain your first down, move the sticks, and extend your play. They will be the deep bomb that will get you over the goal line of global positioning, and gain a sustained competitive advantage.

There is one caveat in achieving this goal line, complacency. Businesses who assume that they can run on automatic pilot once they are on the right road are gravely mistaken. Determination to be the benchmark of success and utilizing continuous quality improvement processes will be the doorstop that will assist in preventing over confidence and lethargic creep. Falling asleep at the wheel especially in a very aggressive market based economy of ever changing trends and consumer tastes, will suddenly send you spiraling down hill. The processes in this book are not a one-time fix with no checks and balances in between. These processes need to be consistently monitored and evaluated, as well as a need to change or modify these processes as the markets and the economy changes. Companies need to consider the goal line only as a measuring stick and not an end to a means. I have witnessed sports venues where the competition was so far out in front that lethargic creep entered in, and defeat was snatched from the jaws of victory. This is a very complex and multi-structured economy consisting of: down falls of the currencies in the European Union, wars, strife in oil rich countries that destabilize markets worldwide, and strikes and protests that can affect manufacturing on an aggregate level.

This is not a market for the faint of heart; however, it is also a market that you cannot afford to ignore. Being successful in these markets is crossing the goal line. Remember, it is only the beginning. Every company must have a plan, a goal, and a measuring rod if you want to track and gage your successes and failures as a means to guide sustainability. I discussed in an earlier chapter the monitoring and evaluating of the functionality of departments as a means of meeting the strategic goals and initiatives of the company. This monitoring and evaluating internally is only a microcosm of the overall evaluating that will need to be monitored.

I intentionally began this chapter discussing the business ethics that will need to be adopted across the board to extend your business play in the marketplace. Without these ethics and best business practices, there is no need to have a strategic plan in place. Ethics in business is the glue that will seal all the rest together. Along with this process, you will also need to have and maintain employee engagement, and have reward systems and promotional opportunities in place to promote leadership and employee involvement. No, we are not drifting off course in finding, crossing, and maintaining your goal line, I am just assisting you in building the foundation to achieve it. I stated earlier that if you do not know where you are going any road in the world will take you there. Well that is the problem at times with companies, they do not have a clear vision or brand that they need to accomplish to find a goal line to cross. It is a great plan to be all things to all people and customers; however, introspectively you need to examine the resources, capital, and factors of production that you have in order to reach your success. I have a domino theory of setting a brand and goal, and it should be to establish your products or services, formulate your brand, acquire the necessary employees, management, and visionaries, and set your goals. Lastly, in this domino list is modify and change as necessary. I call this the domino strategy because conversely in the aforementioned list, if one would fall they could all fall. Let us discuss a little further about establishing a brand and introspection. The global market has a huge treasure of opportunities to offer all companies venturing into the business arena, but from a branding and comparative advantage, are they all yours to be taken? Well, in some respects not all that glitters is gold. Companies are salivating at the many opportunities that are rising in the domestic and global markets inclusive of emerging markets, with a booming economy in China, and the trending of Westernization in the European theater. The opportunities are limitless, yet is your company in a position to dive in or are they just positioning themselves to appear to be the one of the elite group of global players? This is where introspection needs to set in, and self-evaluation becomes a necessity. George Washington knew that he was outmanned and was at a deficit in the Revolutionary War against the mighty British Empire. In this fog of war theater, George Washington did not attempt to pretend that he was the equal to the mighty British troops and weaponry. He attacked with vision, leadership, and a keen and clear vision of the whole battle theater. George Washington attacked using a strategy where he played his strengths in little battles, and continued to beat down the British like a boxer with little jabs and punches. Harkening back to my earlier chapter on Minimum Human Capital--Maximum results, these processes need to be tweaked to play in the global arena according to the size and risk aversion of your company. Using the age-old strategy of comparative and competitive advantage, like a warrior, you need to size up the domestic and global market and attack where you have the advantage.

Thus applying these principles, you will gain ground and get your foot in the door. This will provide your company with a better clear sailing of the horizon in sight.

Let me get back to the comparative advantage principle. When your company is looking over the possibilities of entering the global marketplace, or even a new upstart looking at the possibilities domestically and internationally, there can be no knee jerk reaction to your decision making process. You need to look at your company or business from 30,000 feet. What is your comparative advantage that will put you in the running to capture these markets? Looking over your business model and your branding philosophies, where can you position and leverage your best assets and qualities? You will need to survey the niches of the terrain and make the decision where your team can create a home field advantage with the opportunities. Now, you will need to realize that you cannot put a size 12 foot in a size 10 shoe. In other words, do not force a competency where it will not fit in your attempt to be a giant slayer. Cherry picking at times in a sports scenario may get a bad rap; however, in business selecting your products, services, and markets is a wise decision. Remember, in a next generation economy ever growing needs present a huge opportunity for domestic and international growth. I expressed in earlier chapters that urgency to enter these market niches is imperative, however, selection is necessary. Focus on your direction, examine your strengths, and win the little battles in the marketplace. Assembling these processes will prevent over exposure when the resources are still in the infancy stage.

24 CROSSING THE GOAL LINE

Well congratulations, you crossed the goal line and scored. Your management, employees, and the executives high above in the ivory tower are elated. I can almost visualize the high fives all around as the news circulates of the banner year the company had. Annual Report looks great, investors and stakeholders are happy, and your stock dividends are being paid. Ok, the business world could not have wrote a better script, however, there is a second part to this success and this is where determination and muscle flexing needs to be inserted here. Are you confused? Well, not if you have been following the success script of this book. What is next you may say, we scored! Well, just like a football game there is four quarters to keep competing, the bad news is that in business the game does not end. Everyday is a new beginning and there will be new challenges on the horizon in this great global marketplace. The reason for inviting these issues back to the pages of this book is to recondition the titans of industry to a spirit of vigilance as opposed to the celebratory environments that can once again bring complacency. I am not opposed in anyway to self aggrandizement, yet in this next generation economy with consistent changes driving the market, the end zone dance needs to be one and done, and you must continue to extend the play.

Now, let us look and see how we can stabilize this ever-changing business environment from thirty thousand feet. Many daily changes will surface in this next generation economy that will present the fog of business war even if you were the champion of the year on Wall Street. Let us take a hard look at the many economic and environmental business changes that can take place as the economy changes constantly and dramatically in many areas. From a financial perspective, many challenges are abruptly facing off with your business on a daily basis. In years past, the financial markets used to be primarily domestic in nature; however, with businesses now acting on a global stage, one ripple in the European financial waters can create a tsunami on an aggregate level. Direct business investments in international opportunities can be a tremendous asset when the waters are smooth, however, an internal coup, a destabilized government, civilian protesting over government policies, socio-economic and unemployment concerns all effect European, Asian, and emerging markets as well as Wall Street. These issues all send tremors through the financial world of business that can put tremendous pressure on businesses needing to borrow money as well as staggering currency fluctuations. These financial market jitters coming from the other side of the pond also have a drastic effect on the USA markets.

In a global market, there is not an immunity vaccine to provide a quick remedy outside of your own preparation and vigilance. Highlighting on the financial potholes can be a trip wire to your continued success and prosperity. It is highly necessary to provide some safeguards to stabilize your corporate environment till the storm passes. While your company sails and navigates on the high waters of global foot printing, there will be many financial rough seas and rogue waves that will buffet and hit your corporate ship. First, the financial leaders and visionaries of your company will need to stay awake at the wheel and give careful attention to investments and cash flows, and where they are being targeted. Continue to make certain that cash reserves and cash liquidity are in excess, and not be heavily leveraged in assets and inventories. This is basic home economics that can be applied to a company statement of cash flows. Maintain the best financial eyes on your books and do not get overly creative with the numbers. While this reset economy has a purpose to stabilize the current lack of stability in the economic system, asteroids out of the sky do not stop on a dime. With this in mind, companies need to strap on the safety belt of conservatism with their spending habits, and risk needs to be viewed in a non-myopic atmosphere. Having financial visionaries and wizards always on the lookout for dynamic changes within the economic system, must provide real time information on variable market changes. This needs to be consistently done during the good times in conjunction with prudent spending to garnish cash reserves in excess to pay down debt and keep the ship right sized. Maintain patience with your strategic planning and allow the rogue wave to pass. Remember, after the rain comes the rainbow.

Moving on to a next business challenge that may require you to recondition your strategic planning comes in the form of CUSTOMER SERVICE. Did you take notice that I capitalized these words? That was of course intentional, as I want to highlight the importance of this issue. During the last few years of a bad economy, and as it appears now to be in a continuous downward spiral, maintaining and growing your client base including vendors and suppliers may require a plethora of strategic thought, training, and planning. When there was smooth sailing all hands were on deck, however, when the proverbial economic rogue wave hit, how many went overboard for one reason or the other. In your external environment this reset economy came uninvited into the internal strategies and philosophies of customers and clients. Not only did this specter haunt your customers, but it also invited itself into the solace of your very own corporate culture.

Throughout this book, I continue to emphasize the vital importance of knowing not only the corporate culture that you are doing business with, but also the ethnic, religious, and worldwide cultures that you are facilitating within your global business arena. With that said businesses all realize that pricing of products and services play a vital role in a challenging economy, yet keeping a close eye on the changing needs of your customers is paramount to your success. Taking your customers for granted with an auto pilot mentality is setting a plan for failure. The competition is in search of your clients each and everyday like cold air slipping through the cracks wooing them with promises of superior services and with a steady 'we will be there presence'. Do not think for a moment that there is an allegiance to one business partner, one company, one supplier, or vendor. Speaking candidly, that is why you must be on your toes daily seeking out and presenting new products and services to your customer base as well as new target markets. There is a golden role to maintaining and satisfying your customers and it starts with a call or visit just to say thank you for your business in a very unpretentious manner with no hooks or bait. Just making a visit to see how your services and service levels are making a positive effect on their business needs, and assuring them that you are there to offer any corrections that need attention can be a remedy to success in a cost conscious aggressive environment. Establishing and building this relationship with your customers must also be examined from a product level as well. A business has a due diligence to continue to grow and develop new product sets and service offerings that can be vital to the longevity of your clients or your relationship is a one-way street. This is to be considered a hybrid relationship because your business will be promoting your own longevity as well as that of your customers. You need to perform a market trend analysis of the needs of your customers and target markets as a way of determining what will assist them in the form of new products or services, as well as what offerings will assist them in adding value to their current products. You are now a full-blown customer service model. You not only provide your customers with products, services, and a caring attitude, you are now assisting them with new offerings that will extend their play in the market where many players are competing.

Now, we addressed the external environments of customer service as well as remedies to overcome the singular concept of pricing wars. Now let us peek inside the corporate environs to see how our Human Capital is reacting to the strategies in place to grow and maintain customers. This effort is not a solo act, it takes a total company effort to achieve and grow an environment that will transcend the walls of your brick and mortar building to spread this good will to your customers.

Let us now examine cultural considerations when it comes to customer service. I can now hear the groans of boredom entering in, but not so fast. The reader is more then likely thinking that I have been cultured beyond my expectations and by now, I am a grade A student. My company has promoted diversity awareness, cultural sensitivity, working with and learning intercultural communications, and promoted programs of inclusiveness. What's next? Well, let me now take you to the next cultural sensitivity that you may need to recondition and reinvent with your company as the economy shifts and recreates itself. This is the cultural sensitivity of the changes taking place in the business models and branding that may have taken place with your current base of customers. This can be a very convoluted problem that will require much attention and critical thinking processes. This cultural change needs to be addressed to all employees across the board from the receptionist to the management and beyond. This needs to be framed as not being business as usual, as your clients may have gone through dramatic changes in management, products, and services, as well as philosophical changes and business style. New staff may have taken on roles that formerly were held by individuals you knew for years. So with possible changes in products and services, there will possibly be changes in human capital were you will need to make adjustments. Speaking formerly on critical thinking processes, this will need to be addressed with articulation and attention to detail. Now one caveat, this may not take place with all your clients, but this is the red flag that I would like to send up for preparation that needs to be made. Another caveat, this process may need examined across multiple customers, and not only customers, but vendors and suppliers as well. I believe that companies are parochial in their thinking where customer service needs are concerned. Mostly, it is pointed toward communications such as answering the phone, addressing customer concerns, and facilitating complaints. On the surface this is necessary, however, in a next generation economy joining forces with a reset economy this makes for the perfect storm forming a rogue wave that can broadside your business.

Now here is where the real complexities can take center stage because as you attempt to facilitate the external market changes harnessing your customers, you may be taking on the same changes with you own business. Now we have a real issue that will take on the Darwin theory of survival of the fittest. Do you remember this from my earlier chapters? Ok! Enough already may be your response to this situation. Talk about the fog of business wars, this environment of complexities can be a total fog out. What do you do then to resolve this customer service dilemma? First, do not under use your knowledge people, nor in a tough economy make them expendable during cost cutting measures. Recall that in earlier chapters I discussed auditing the functionality of your departments across the board, well now this process needs to take place fast and furious and with total attention to the market and your internal and external customers. Now, before moving forward, I constantly and consistently addressed that each department needs to focus steadily on the trends and changes in the market and economic changes taking place. This is vital to extending your play and eliminating the impact of the economic rogue waves that can come out of nowhere. Preparation can turn a tsunami into a rainstorm. Every department needs a visionary leader with their finger on the pulse of the current business environment, as well as on the pulse of your customers, vendors, and suppliers. Is this a challenge? In a word, yes. Is this process and plan able to be accomplished? Most definitely, if you carry out all the steps with due diligence. Now here is the upside to all of this, this plan is customizable and can be utilized by small businesses as well as large corporations. It will take a little tweaking and a little massaging, but the beauty is that the principles of business sustainability are pretty much in conformity across the board.

Ok, let's move on. Realizing the changing needs of your customers can be a difficult chore if you do not analyze and take the correct proactive approach to discovery. Now calling every customer is a tremendous asset to that approach as it will not only build relationships, but will promote an era of good feeling. This call cannot only be a good feeling call, but a call of genuine concern and of establishing a parallel universe with your client. Have you ever thought of that concept, establishing a parallel universe and the reason behind this? This is a concept of taking on the vision and strategy of your customer in order to plan your own strategy of sustainability.

I stated earlier that it may be very difficult for large corporate concerns to contact every customer, vendor, and supplier, but it is necessary and has to be done. To ease the burden, you will need to create little economies of scale with your marketing and research and development team, to utilize their expertise on examining market trends and new product development that will assist in knowing a collective group of your customers and their needs. I stated earlier that it is your due diligence to know your customers, and understand their product and service needs to the point that you will be their provider and their consultant. This will put you one jump ahead of your competition, and this will be your brand and business model.

In my earlier chapter on the leadership of George Washington, I mentioned that he helped his troops to see the heat of battle through the eyes of his leadership and vision. Even in the direst moments, they saw the light at the end of the tunnel and reacted on it. Even in the fog of war, they were able to navigate and be successful. Why was this? Your business needs to know the reason why, and draw up a strategic blueprint that is focused and flexible. This is the plan that you need to service your customers, build a relationship, form a parallel universe, act as a product and service consultant, and constantly find ways to promote new products and services in a very lean manufacturing process to add value and cost effectiveness. We are still viewing from thirty thousand feet, however, now we have to drop down a bit to get an inside view of your internal customers, your human capital. When the next generation economy ripples changes through the domestic and global business arena, your culture and processes may have to change as well. This is the next challenge that I would like to address that may need to be reset or reconditioned, however, let us first look at the internal culture that may dramatically sneak in and disturb your inner tranquility. Events in the economy can broadside attitudes, and impose a very nasty negative attitude if not controlled and harnessed immediately. This is also part of that fog of business war from an introspective view. When a person is not feeling well on the inside, it is eventually reflected on the outside no matter how much you attempt to conceal it. In a sporting event, you may have heard at times that the opposing team was performing so well that it took the wind and game plan of the other team right out the window. Well this is how a reset and regressive economy can affect your team internally.

Let's move on to the explanation and correction. One constant in life is change, and as I stated in an earlier chapter on corporations needing to be organic or die, you can expect change to always take place. In our human capacity change always brings about a certain amount of stress. Change is an unknown until it is clearly defined and exposed. This is true in our personal lives as well as in the life of a corporation. Economic downturns, losses in financial stability, and at the worse a total loss of business can be devastating to your human capital as this hits like a hybrid affecting their work life balance. For beginners, let us take a look at how these stressors can wreak havoc on management, and how it can spiral out of control. Management has a huge grid of executives above it pulling the strings and evaluating the performance levels. The strategy that was set forth on the white board in the ivory tower will need to be constantly monitored and evaluated. Management is highly accountable for the drive and the results of this strategy, and this can be a very daunting task in a down economy as well as a very stressful situation. This perfect storm can take place when a severe amount of strain is placed on the employee base causing work loss issues, attitude problems, and a drop in morale from a hybrid of management and performance pressures. Job security also enters the picture as employees and management get the strained neck syndrome from consistently looking over their shoulders. Now you may ask, what does this have to do with customer service? Just about everything. Like the smell of natural gas, it permeates throughout the entire organization. Employees and management find it very difficult to focus on customer service when they feel that their company and jobs are taking on water, and it may be a battle for survival to maintain both. Now here is where the water really gets murky. Let us add in more challenges to the mix like adapting and facilitating the ever-changing needs of your customers, getting new products to market to beat the competition, and all the while needing to be acclimated to the ever-changing diversity in the human capital base internally and externally. Mission impossible? Not really. Hard work and determination, you bet. Now that we have discussed taking corrective action with this kind of a problem, it will require a very concise and methodical plan working in concert with each other. Now, no one can solve what is unknown, so we already know that communication will be a vital ingredient in the recipe to facilitate these customer service challenges. I discussed in previous chapters the importance of transparency from the top to the bottom figuratively speaking. All things being equal, the only constant is change and change can be a constant form of stress in humanity. Knowing the thunderstorms are created when forces collide, it is harnessing these forces adequately that calms the storm. Communication is vital throughout the entire organization bringing into light what is unknown, and making transparent what is not visible. Employees can adjust to various situations when they know what is happening and what is expected. Just as when you are driving a long distance, and monitoring the weather as you go, you can make adjustments to your travel plans to avoid precarious situations.

Let's begin with the aspects of total communication, and how this will keep the equilibrium within the corporation. From a personal standpoint, I have seen drastic changes in companies from layoffs, to cutbacks, to total buyouts, and believe me the information was never communicated to the employees that these situations were going to take place, and why they were happening. I am quite sure that you know the results of this culture and what takes place during the guesswork. The employees without the necessary information start to formulate opinions and conjectures as to what may be taking place as something does not seem right within the system. Like a ship taking on water, the rumor mill begins to take effect and the employees start to jump off board. Some other symptoms of this contagion is cut back on productivity, frequent call offs, and management and employee clashes taking place. The corrective process that could have remedied this whole situation was for management to take the reins and speak to the employees about upcoming necessary changes and evaluations that will be taking place to try to remain sustainable and competitive in a reset economy. The invitation for employee feedback to address concerns, as well as informing them of infrastructure changes and the retooling that will be taking place can produce fantastic results. Will all be satisfied with the changes? Of course not, but leaving the employees in the dark is not a plan to succeed. This ambience of communication and transparency will demonstrate a culture of care and concern for your employee base and produce positive results. Just getting all on board with the new functionality of the revitalized or restructured system can bring amazing results. Eliminating the haze of change will assist in eliminating the forces of inertia. I want to take this theory a step further. I believe that when the brass and management while continually keeping their finger on the pulse of the business arena senses a change in the normal course of business, should keep employees abreast of the changes and necessary actions that need to be actuated. This is communication and transparency working in harmony to stimulate success.

Let us now examine the oxygen tank of the corporation, which is training and development. In an earlier chapter, I discussed how the human capital is the plasma or lifeblood of the company, well at times the blood needs a little pumping in the form of training and development. I have heard employees in various companies discuss how they were just told to facilitate a job and its essential functions with no training prior to filling the position. I believe that during a serious decline in the economy and budgets getting low in the tank, training can take a back seat, making way for quick production and a just get it done attitude. With the competition in the marketplace, this is a set up for failure. Look at the maze that companies have to go through just to remain competitive in a global market with a diverse culture of employees. This training now has to undertake a dual personality as it becomes and internal and external affair. In the past, after the strategy was set, training mostly became an internal self-feeding organism. The game plan was set on the white board in the C Suite and disseminated to management who became the watchdog over the employees to carry out the plan.

In this next generation economy, the employees need to have unfettered access to as many strategically crafted training programs as possible. You may say that this is definitely a financial burden on the financial expenditures used for training spend, however, the ROI will be fantastic. These are necessary dollars that cannot be eliminated, and if needed review the chapter on training and development to craft the training programs to meet your strategy in the most economical format. Therefore, to summarize this corrective action needed to address customer service from a training and development perspective, marketing, research and development, finance, and human resources, will all need to be trained in a hybrid format with internal and external customers in mind. Trend analysis on your customers, new product development, and carefully crafted financial planning needs to be addressed according to the needs of your internal and external customers and market. Spare no expense.

We never enter into business with an intent to fail, yet at times we fail to plan, and that immediately brings about the downfall of what could be a successful venture into the global business market. I have developed the processes in this book to stimulate your business logistics beyond the norm and lead you to think outside of the brick and mortar C Suite mentality. The C Suite can be a great think tank of strategic positioning and leveraging of corporate competencies and comparative advantages, however, at times in the day-to-day operations the navigation system gets lost in the fog of daily business wars while the ever-changing details and trends get lost in regimentation and obscurity in the delegated grid process. With this said, I want to revitalize the necessity of constant real time and consistent clear information that will keep the stream running smoothly. Realistically there is no magic potion that auto-corrects any mistakes and pitfalls in the daily business operations, however, I have brought to light stop gap processes to put into place that will avoid major cataclysmic events. I still need to reinforce the fact that consistent vigilance and trend analysis needs to be two daily ingredients that will promote sustainability. Wrap this up with superior business ethics, visionary leadership, and employee empowerment and you now have the recipe to EXTEND THE PLAY.

ABOUT THE AUTHOR

Terry has an MBA and a Bachelor of Science degree in International Business. He is an Adjunct Professor teaching in the areas of Performance Management, Organizational Training and Development, and Human Resources Management. He also possesses over 20 years of experience in the Public and Private Sectors. Terry currently resides in Pennsylvania with his wife, and enjoys sports, International traveling, and reading.